Over Sexteen

PRUDES WON'T THINK IT FUNNY!

WILDSIDE PRESS

He who has
an evil mind

is a Dirty Dog

PROLOGUE

It's tough to find
    for love or money,
a joke that's clean
    and also funny.

Sex is the subject matter behind most of these anec-
dotes. However, the average person does not laugh
because of any lewdness in the story but rather at
the ridiculousness of the situation. People do not
laugh at words, they laugh at themselves.

The contents of this book is a compilation of stories
and cartoons that appeared in "ABSEER", the
house organ of the ABC Freight Forwarding Cor-
poration. We make no pretense at originality. The
droll material printed in the "ABSEER" was derived
from the contributions of its many readers. "Over
Sexteen" is really a collection of jokes that have
undoubtedly been heard around the world. Humor,
like history, repeats itself. Yet every joke is new to
some one and many are worth repeating. But "Over
Sexteen" is not composed of stories alone, it contains
choice cartoons, cartoons with animation, brought
to life by the gifted brush of Bruce Dolen.

"Over Sexteen" is recommended for the intelligent
adult, who, unless he or she is a prude, will more
than likely enjoy most of these pages.

This is the beginning. For all we know, it may also
be the end. Our waste baskets are full, our pockets
are empty. The rest, dear readers, is up to you.

J. M. Elgart
Editor

LIMERICKS

There was a young lady named Ransom
Who was loved three times in a hansom.
But when she asked for more
Came a weak voice from the floor,
My name is Simpson—not Sampson.

Once there was a queer named Broom
Who invited a girl (?) to his room;
They argued all night
As to who had the right
To do what, with which and to whom.

There once was a girl from Madras
Who had a most beautiful ass
It wasn't pink
As you might think
But grey, had long ears, and ate grass.

Little Johnny, with a grin
Drank up all of pappy's gin.
Mother said, when he was plastered
"Go to bed, you little love-child."

Mary had an aeroplane
In it she loved to frisk
Wasn't she a silly girl
Her little *

There was a young lady from France
Who thought that she'd just "take a chance."
For an hour or so, she just "let herself go."
And now all her sisters are aunts!

"Boy! This is going to be some hell of a play."

AN L OF A TIME A couple on a blind date visited the carnival grounds at a local park. They went for a ride on the merry-go-round. The ride completed, she seemed kinda bored. "Now what would you like to do?" he asked "I'd like to be weighed," she replied. So he took her over to the weight guesser. "107," the man said — and he was absolutely right.

Then they rode on the whip, after which he again asked her what she would like to do. "I wanna get weighed," was again her answer.

"There's a screw loose here somewhere," thought Paul, so he took the babe on back home even if it wasn't yet ten o'clock.

And the gal's mother, noting that she was home un-usually early, said to her, "What's the matter, Dear? Didn't you have a good time?"

"Wousy," came back the answer.

TIES IN A woman was shopping for a pair of pants for her little boy. "Do you want knickers with a zipper?" asked the clerk. "No, Johnnie has a sweater with a zipper and he's always getting his tie caught in it," was the reply.

KEEP TRYING A woman got on the train with nine children, and when the conductor came for her tickets she said: "Now these children are thirteen years old and pay full fare, but those three over there are only six and these three here are four and a half."

The conductor looked at her in astonishment. "Do you mean to say you get three every time?" he asked. "Oh, no," she said. "Sometimes we don't get any at all."

"As soon as he came poking around with his old cold nose . . . I let him have it . . ."

DOG TAGS? Some of the girls were seated on the porch of the club-house at the golf course. Somehow, the locker room door was partly open and the girls could not help but notice a nude man whose head and shoulders were covered by a bath towel.

After studying the body, so to speak, one of the girls reported that it was not her husband. A second girl gazed at the man and said, "No, it isn t my husband." Then a third girl, who was a life-of-the-party type, shifted her chair, peered intently at the masculine torso and blurted, "Why, he isn't even a member of the club!"

REAL GONE A flea frolicking in a meadow was swallowed by a bull. "I'll revenge myself on this nasty beast as soon as I have rested up," vowed the flea to itself, and took a nap. When the flea awoke, the bull was gone.

ALL WET Lee Frankfurter was sitting in the bar of a downtown hotel. Seated next to him was a gentleman who had definitely had enough and was surveying his empty glass. Something seemed to be decidedly wrong with him and presently he turned to Lee and asked,

"Shay, didjou shpill a glass of beer on me?"

"Certainly not!" answered Lee.

The souse turned to the man on his other side.

"Mishter, didjou by any chance throw a glass of beer in my lap?"

"No!" snapped the man.

The drunk mulled over this information.

"Jusht what I been sushpectin'," he declared. "It'sh an inside job!"

"I am *not!*"

GONE BUT NOT FORGOTTEN The preacher decided to enumerate the Ten Commandments to his flock. When he got to the fourth, "Thou Shalt Not Steal," he noticed a fellow in the first row acting nervously. When the preacher got to the seventh, "Thou Shalt Not Commit Adultery," he noticed the fellow suddenly brighten up and smile. After the service, the preacher approached the man and asked him the reason for his unseemly conduct. To which the happy one replied, "When you told the Fourth Commandment, 'Thou Shalt Not Steal,' I discovered my umbrella was gone. But when you said, 'Thou Shalt Not Commit Adultery,' I remembered where I had left it."

RECAST Hollywood humor we read some place:
There was a married couple and they were accompanied every place by the husband's best friend.
One day the wife died and at the funeral the grief-stricken bachelor carried on hysterically.
Finally the husband started to console him.
"Take it easy, John, take it easy," he said. "I'll get married again."

SO-LUNG Winter, snow, sleet, etc. conjures up thoughts of sunny climes; and this young man keeps talking about a vacation at Miami Beach. He tells about his last visit there, when, with a friend (a noted physician who specializes in ailments of the lungs), he lay on the beach admiring the surrounding beauty or beauties. He turned to his friend and said, "The girls at these Florida beaches have beautiful legs, haven't they?" To which the lung specialist replied, "I hadn't noticed; I'm a chest man myself!"

"This is the Arabian Broadcasting Company, bringing to you your favorite Quiz program 'YOU BET YOUR ASS.' "

SUNNYSIDE UP The charming young lady who submitted the following story insists it's true.

She happened to be in a lingerie shop and couldn't help overhearing a man trying to buy a brassiere for his wife. This man obviously didn't realize it was necessary to know the size, but the friendly saleslady tried to help him out of his difficulty.

"How about the size of grapefruit?" she asked.

"No, smaller," replied the customer.

"About like oranges?" hopefully asked the saleslady.

"No, smaller," he answered.

"Then, how about eggs," suggested the clerk.

"Yeah, yeah," said the man, "fried."

OUT FRONT The young thing was sitting on her front porch knitting some tiny garments. And her mother said to a neighbor: "I'm glad to see that she has taken an interest in something other than running around with boys."

LOGICAL A young father was shopping at a department store with his daughter, when the little girl suddenly said, "Daddy, I gotta go."

"Not right now," replied the father.

"I gotta go now," shouted the girl.

To avoid a crisis, a saleslady stepped up and said: "That's all right, sir, I'll take her."

The saleslady and the little girl went off hurriedly, hand in hand. On their return, Tony looked at his daughter and said: "Did you thank the nice lady for being so kind?"

"Why should I thank her?" retorted the little girl, "She had to go, too."

Over
Sexteen

UNTRUE A woman approached the pearly gates and spoke to Saint Peter.

"Do you know if my husband is here? His name is Smith."

"Lady, we have lots of them here, you'll have to be more specific."

"Joe Smith."

"Lotsa those too, you'll have to have more identification."

"Well, when he died he said that if I was ever untrue to him, he'd turn over in his grave."

"Oh, you mean 'Pinwheel Smith'."

NO SALE He met his ex-wife at a party and after a few drinks suggested that they have another try at marriage.

She sneered: "Over my dead body."

He sneered: "I see you haven't changed a bit."

EVEN STEVEN It was quite a swanky bar in the best part of town. The new arrival ordered a bottle of beer. Paying with a dollar bill, he was surprised when the young bartender gave him ninety cents change. When questioned about it, the bartender said that a dime was all he was charging.

The customer being rather hungry, and pleased with the apparent low prices of the place, ordered a ham and cheese sandwich on rye. "That'll be fifteen cents," said the barkeep. The customer's eyes widened—"I can't understand it. How can you sell stuff so low?" he asked.

"Listen, buddy," said the bartender, "I just work here. I'm not the boss. He's upstairs with my wife and I'm doing the same thing to him down here."

"Great Heavens Paul!"

HOBO NEWS A hobo was cruising along the Bowery in a brand new Cadillac convertible. Some friends stopped him and wanted to know how in the world he got that car. The man behind the wheel explained:

"I was sitting on the curb minding my own business when a beautiful girl pulled up in this car that you see. 'Want a ride?' she asked. So I got in. We rode far out into the country and she stopped the car. We both got out. 'Kiss me,' she said. So I kissed her. She was really a beautiful doll. Then she started to disrobe and stood there in all her feminine beauty clothed only in a pair of silk panties. Holding her arms out toward me she said, 'You can have anything I've got!'

Well, I could see that her panties would never fit me — so I took the car."

DESPERATE One cold Saturday morning, a suburban resident noticed his neighbor walking in his backyard and wearing only a pajama top, nothing more.

"What's the idea?" inquired the onlooker.

"I don't know," said the neighbor, "the other day I walked over to the drug store without a scarf and got a stiff neck. It's my wife's idea."

FLOORED It seems the elevator operator in a local department store was quite a novice, probably on his first tour. Suddenly, the car was brought to an abrupt stop.

"Did I stop too quickly?" the operator asked the passengers.

"Oh, no, indeed," coolly replied a little old lady in the rear of the car, "I always wear my bloomers down around my ankles."

It seems that one night a young boy took the girl next door into the woods and when questioned about it by his parents, confessed that he had been a bad, bad boy.

"You did wrong, son," said his mother, "but you told the truth and because of that I shall reward you with some cookies."

The following night the same thing happened. Again his mother told him he had done wrong but because he was truthful she gave him some cookies. On the third night, history was repeating itself when the father left the room.

"Where are you going, Pa?" asked his wife.

"I'm going into the kitchen to fry a few eggs, the lad can't keep that up on cookies."

AR PERFORMER Billie: "What are you doing with that letter on your sweater? Don't you know you're not supposed to wear that unless you've made the team?"

Millie: "Well?"

HARDLY A Texas preacher was haranguing his congregation on the subject of sin. He grew more and more eloquent and finally shouted, "Is dey one single virgin in this congregation? If dey is let her stand up!" He then paused, nobody stood up. He was about to resume when he noticed a young woman standing in the rear of the church with a baby in her arms. "Scuse me, young lady, did you understand the question? I asked was dere a virgin in the house."

"Yes Sah," says the mother, "but you don't expect this 3 weeks old girl baby to stand by herself, does you?"

SAVOIR FAIRE Three Frenchmen were discussing the meaning of savoir faire. The first explained: "If you come home and discover your wife in another man's arms and you say 'Excuse me,' that's savoir faire."

"No, no," said another who was slightly older than the first, "that's not quite right. Savoir faire is if you come home and find your wife in another man's arms and you say 'Excuse me, proceed.' That's savoir faire."

The third Frenchman was still older and wiser, and he said gravely, "No, my sons, neither of you quite understands the meaning. If you come home and discover your wife in the arms of another man and you say 'Excuse me, proceed' and he proceeds, he has savoir faire."

PRECOCIOUS The children of the third grade were going to draw pictures, and write letters to boys and girls in foreign countries. The teacher gave out names and addresses, and one little boy got a girl in Holland for a pen pal.

That night he breezed into the house, and said cheerfully, "Guess what, Mom? I got a girl in Dutch!"

MAN OR MOUSE Red Diamond was having lunch with a young fellow who announced his engagement. "Tonight," said Red, "will decide whether you're a man or a mouse. If you make love to her tonight, you're a man. If you're afraid to assert yourself and put off the happy day, you are just a mouse."

"I guess I'm a rat," said the young man sadly, "I made love to her *last* night."

"Can't unnerstan' it. Damn thing's been runnin'
for hours."

ONCE UPON Once a king, always a king but
Once a knight's enough.

MARK X'S THE SPOT Cleopatra and Mark Anthony were floating down the River Nile on her flower-bedecked barge. Cleopatra was lying on a couch; Anthony was standing before her orating.

"Cleopatra," he said, "love for you surges through me like a raging forest fire that consumes the country-side. Furthermore, O Goddess of the Nile—"

"Mark," Cleo interrupted impatiently, "I am not prone to argue."

TEMPUS FUGIT She got out of bed,
Put on her robe,
Put up the shade,
Uncovered the parrot,
Went to the kitchen
Lit the gas,
Put on the coffee,
And the telephone rang.
"Hi-ya Babe, just got in from St. Paul
Get ready and I'll be right over."
She took off the coffee,
Turned off the gas,
Went into the bedroom
Pulled down the shade,
Covered the parrot,
Took off the robe,
Got in the bed,
And the parrot said,
"Mighty damn short day, wasn't it?"

"Good evening, Madam."

BRIEF A group of Scotchmen dressed in traditional kilts, were part of a parade that was temporarily held up because of traffic. A woman standing on the curb spoke to one of the costumed paraders, saying, "Excuse me for being curious, but I've always wondered what you wore under those short kilts."

The Scotchman looked at her for a moment with cocked eyebrow and answered, "I'm a man of few words. Give me your hand."

SALE A traveling buyer had been on a trip for three months. Every few weeks he'd send a telegram to his wife saying: "Can't come home. Still buying." The wife stood it for a while, but when the fourth month started and her husband still had no idea of returning, she decided to do something. She sent him a telegram. "Better come home. I'm selling what you're buying."

MISPLACED "Did you follow my advice about kissing your girl friend when she least expected it?"

"Oh darn," said the lad with the swollen eye, "I didn't know you said *when,* I thought you said *where.*"

GEOGRAPHY OF WOMEN

16-22   like Africa part virgin, part explored.
23-35   like Asia dark and mysterious.
36-45   like United States high tone and technical.
46-55   like Europe devastated but still interesting in places.
60 —   like Australia—everybody knows about it, but nobody goes there.

NO HAITCH? The fair village was all agog over the annual spelling bee. One by one the contestants dropped out and even our fair schoolmarm was eliminated when she stumbled over "psittacosis."

At last only two remained, the village druggist and the stableman, who was an Englishman.

They waited eagerly for the word. It came:

"How do you spell 'auspice'?"

The stableman lost.

DOWN MEMORY LANE Reporter: "To what do you attribute your old age?"

95-year-old-woman: "I've eaten moderately, I work hard, I do not drink or smoke and I keep good hours."

Reporter: "Have you ever been bedridden?"

Old Woman: "Yes, sure I have, but don't put that in the paper."

CHANGEABLE "Your feet are cold," he complained to his little bride, "keep them on your own side of the bed."

She began to sob. "You're cruel," she cried, "you never used to say that to me before we were married!"

BROOKLYN BLEND An avid Dodger fan relates a humorous incident at the World Series Game he attended.

Right after the game, he went to the men's room and the famous Leo Durocher was just coming out. In a moment he found himself inside, standing alongside a youngster who turned his head upward, grinned broadly and said: "Right on top of Leo Durocher's!"

"I just put all I had on Johnstown!"

HOMEWORK   A traveling salesman who was not feeling up to snuff, visited his doctor for a check-up. A routine examination did not reveal any particular ailment. The doctor then questioned his patient about his living habits. "Now I'm going to get personal," said the doc, "how often do you engage in sexual relationship?"

"Every Monday, Wednesday and Friday, regularly," replied the other.

"Well," went on the doctor, "Your trouble may lie there. I prescribe you eliminate the Wednesdays."

"Oh, no," answered the salesman, "I couldn't do that. That's the only night of the week I'm home."

BUTT DEFINITELY   One of our elder professors can't wait until the lecture permits him to define a fairy. Hereafter students will recognize such a person as someone who likes his vice versa.

NIGHT OF NIGHTS   They had been married that afternoon in Minneapolis and journeyed to the distant city of St. Paul where they had a room at a downtown hotel. Night had fallen and the bride had already donned the beautiful silken nightie reserved for this occasion and was lounging voluptuously upon the bed. For over an hour now, the groom, still fully dressed, had been gazing out the open window into the darkness. Impatiently Gladys addressed him. "Why don't you undress, dear, and come to bed?"

"Never mind me," he replied. "Go ahead and go to sleep. My mother told me this would be the most wonderful night I'd ever see and I don't want to miss a single minute of it!"

"I just got laid!"

WHAT, NO SKIS?   A soldier just returned from three years overseas arrived at a camp near his home town. He was naturally very anxious to see his wife, but try as he would, he could not possibly wangle over two hours' leave. After six hours' absence, he came back to camp. "Why the hell are you four hours A.W.O.L.?" barked his sergeant. "Well, you see," said the soldier, "When I got home I found my wife in the bathtub and it took me four hours to dry out my uniform."

STUBBORN   The subject of modern-day morality was debated with much earnestness for half an hour between the young lady and her date. The date put forth the dictum that it was possible to take advantage of a young lady at will, whether she chose to permit it or not. The maiden was firm in maintaining that such was not the case.

Finally it was decided that the only solution to the question was by a practical demonstration. So they tried it. They clinched and the battle was on. After a lively tussle her date proved his point.

The gal showed an undaunted spirit. "O, well, you didn't win fair," argued the young lady, "my foot slipped there on that little rug. Let's try it again!"

QUICK   A slightly obese man had taken a prominent seat in a street car. A woman sitting opposite, noticed him and whispered to her lady friend:

"If that stomach was on a woman it would indicate that she was in a family-way."

The man overhead the remark. He smiled back gently, and said:

"Lady, it was; and she is!"

FAIRY TALE A girl was walking along a country road and almost stepped on a frog. She was about to go on when the frog began to speak.

"I have not always been a frog," he croaked, "I was once a tall, dark, handsome man but was transformed into this creature you now see by a wicked and magical genie. The spell can only be broken if I spend a night under the pillow of a beautiful girl."

The girl, of course, was skeptical but the pleading eyes of the unhappy frog caused her to take him home that night and put him under her pillow.

Sure enough, when she awoke the next morning, there beside her she found a tall, dark, gorgeous hunk of man.

Well, you know, to this very day her mother does not believe that story.

FERRY TALE One of our New Jersey customers found himself in the Times Square section of New York and stopped a flashily dressed young man to ask, "Where can I find the 42nd Street Ferry?"

"Thpeaking," he replied.

FOOLED A languid southern beauty was telling some friends about the mos' interestin' man she'd met the night before.

"He took me up in his place," she said, "and showed me a perfectly huge closet full of the darlingest mink coats you've ever seen — I mean they really were. And he let me take the one I liked best home with me."

"And what did you have to do for it?" asked a friend.

"Just shorten the sleeves, honey!" was the answer.

PHONETIC My little son was doing his homework: "Three plus one, the son of a bitch is four," he was saying. "Three plus two, the son of a bitch is five. Three plus three, the son of a bitch is six," and so on. Horrified, I asked him where on earth he had picked up that language. "Oh, that's the way they teach us at school," he replied.

The following day I went to see his teacher and asked her about it. At first she was equally horrified, then her face broke into a grin. "I get it," she cried, "we teach the children to say, three plus one, the sum of which is four. Three plus two, the sum of which is five."

TAKES TIME Two girls met for lunch and were discussing their marriage prospects. "I hear your boy friend graduates from law school next month. I guess you'll get married then?"

"Oh, no, not right away," answered the other, "I want him to practice about a year first."

CAMPUS CAPERS Peters was the college's star fullback. But a few days before the BIG game he injured his leg in scrimmage, and was told he wouldn't play in THE game of the year. The college paper announced the sad news with this headline—"Team Will Play Without Peters."

The jolly dean, however, spotted this bit of college headline writing before it went to press and gave orders to change it or get kicked off the paper.

The editor changed it, and Saturday morning the paper hit the campus with this headline—"Team Will Play With Peters Out."

GOOD FOR THE GOOSE... Mr. P. Shocks, an irrigation expert, has recently undergone a serious operation, the success of which depended largely upon the process of forced feeding, through the south end looking north.

Free from the effects of the ether and opiates he began to look around and the first thing he discovered was the feeding machine with its tube near his bedside.

"Good Heaven!" he cried out to the nurse, "what's that thing for?"

The nurse gently explained about the feeding.

"All right," said the patient, somewhat pacified, "but I want two more of those machines."

He refused to give a reason for this strange request and finally, in order to quiet him, she had an orderly bring in two more.

"Now," she said, "I wish you would tell me why you want them."

The patient smiled sardonically. "Well," he explained, "you and the doctor have been so darn kind that I want you both to have lunch with me tomorrow."

PANHANDLER When one of our colleagues was confined in a hospital for several weeks, he was served so faithfully by an orderly named Ben that he gave him an unusually large tip the day he got out. Ben was overwhelmed and felt he had to pay a compliment in return. He gulped and uttered, "We're goin' to miss you terribly around here, Sir, you sure take a good enema."

COIN PURLOIN And pie-eyed Pete thinks the meanest guy in the world is the restaurant proprietor who goes around pinching the waitresses' tips.

"Chicken!"

BUXOM   Have you heard of the tragic case of a woman who was determined to end it all? She called on her physician and startled him by asking what was the best way of committing suicide.

"What?" said the medical man, "what on earth do you want to do that for?"

"Never mind, doctor, I've got too much trouble and my mind is made up. If you don't advise me, I'll just jump off a high building or something, so you'd better tell me."

"Well, if you take it that way," he said, "the best thing to do is to go home, undress, go to bed and shoot yourself two inches below the left breast."

The woman took his advice, went home and blew off her knee-cap!

MASTER SERGEANT   A company of women soldiers in England with blouses off, was being inspected by the sergeant when the captain appeared and, seeing what was going on, shouted: "My Gawd, sergeant, what are you doing? I said inspect their kits!"

"Oh," replied the sergeant. "I misunderstood you."

SOB STORY   There's the story about Tony, whose wife passed away and he was almost inconsolable. At the cemetery he collapsed with grief. In the car, riding back home, his whole frame shook with wild sobs.

"Now, now, Tony, my boy," soothed his friend. "It's really not so bad. I know itsa tough now, but in sixa month maybe you find another beautiful bambina and firsta ting you know you getta married again."

Tony turned to him in rage. "Sixa month," he shouted. "What I gonna do tonight?"

"Do you think you'd have time
for a short one?"

LIKE FATHER   When little Johnnie returned home from his first day at school, his mother asked him what he had learned that day.

"Nothing," said Johnnie, "but the teacher asked me something I couldn't answer. She wanted to know if I favored my father or my mother."

"Well," answered his mother, "I suppose she was wondering which of us you resemble. If she asks you again, just tell her that you have your father's features but your eyes are like mine."

Little Johnnie was hardly inside the school room the next morning when he made himself heard. "I can answer your question now, teacher," he shouted, "my eyes are like my mother's, but I have my father's fixtures!"

MADE MAID   The other night when an old maid found a tramp under her bed it so upset her that her stomach was on the bum all night.

POLLY!   An old maid went to a pet shop to purchase a parrot. She wanted a very nice one though. He could talk but he must talk nice. The pet shop owner looked around and said, "I have just the bird you want. This parrot here, as you can see, has a string tied to each leg. Pull the string on his right leg and he recites the Ten Commandments. Pull the string on his left leg and he recites the Lord's Prayer."

The old maid considered for a moment and said, "What happens if I pull both strings?"

"I'd fall on my pratt, you darn fool!" yelled the parrot.

Oh Doctor! What shall I do with these rectal thermometers?"

SHE SAID PLEASE   Three college boys upon entering their favorite juke-joint to sit at their usual table found it to be occupied by an oldish woman. Upon debating what to do about the situation, they finally decided to embarrass the woman into leaving.

Sitting next to the old lady, the first student proceeded, "Say, John," he said, "did you know that I was born three months before my parents were married?"

"Why, that's nothing . . ." said the next one. "I was born six months before my parents were married."

"Fellows," replied the last of the hungry men, "I was born without my parents being married."

The old lady finally looked up from the table and pleasantly said, "Will one of you bastards please pass the salt?"

FAST WORKER   Said the young man about town to the beautiful lady he was dining with that evening;

"Will you have breakfast with me in the morning?" "Sure," she replied. "Then," answered the young man, "shall I phone you, or nudge you?"

VARIETY   In a philosophical discussion about the "hereafter" it is pretty well agreed that the average person believes he would improve himself and do better if he could re-live his life. The case of Adam was brought up. Here was a man who lived in the Garden of Eden but when he reached Heaven he was asked, "Adam, if you had your life to live over again, would you be content to duplicate it?" Adam thought for a moment and replied, "No, if I had my life to live over again, I think I would like to turn over a new leaf."

NEW SWITCH   Ralph and Jack were being hooked at the same time by Anne and Betty respectively. May we repeat, Anne belonged to Ralph and Betty belonged to Jack. The four newly weds spent their honeymoon together at Niagara Falls; they occupied adjoining rooms, sat at the same table and became inseparable — well, almost inseparable. After dinner one evening they started upstairs and as they neared their rooms, lightning struck a transformer and out went the lights! They were in pitch darkness!

Groping around, they made their way into their rooms and quietly undressed for bed. Ralph, a religious fellow, knelt to pray. Just as he completed his prayer, the lights came on and he saw much to his astonishment that it was Betty there in his bed instead of his own wife, Anne. He jumped up and dashed for the door.

"Too late to hurry now," cooed Betty. "Jack never prays."

OFA SO GOOD   "The man who invented the davenport should be a happy man—millions have been made on it."

NNY GRANNY   Mamma, watching daughter dress for a party sez, "Ain't you gonna put on no panties tonight, dear?" "Naw, Ma, hit ain't cold," sez daughter. So mamma, quite perturbed, tells daughter to go ask grandma what she thought about it — so daughter goes upstairs 'n' sez, "Grandmaw — effen you's goes out to have a date with your sweetheart and thought you might have a chance to get kissed — you wouldn't wear no veil, would you?"

"Naw," sez grandmaw, "I sho' wouldn't."

STUFFED CABBAGE During the stay of a small circus in a little town down South, a particularly violent electric storm caused the single elephant of the outfit to "stampede." Next morning, bright and early, the town constable got a call.

"Come out immediately," an excited feminine voice was heard to say, "there is a huge animal of some kind in my garden, and he's pulling up my cabbage with his tail."

"What's he doing with the cabbage?" questioned the officer.

"You wouldn't believe me if I told you," came back the answer.

TOO MUCH BANGING Then there's the bachelor who got thrown out of his apartment when the landlady heard him drop his shoes on the floor twice.

HAYMAKER A very handsome young chap was recently hired in a large accounting firm. In a short while the young man came to Mr. Diamond, his department head and said, "I am sorry to tell you, but some of the young ladies in this office are tempting me sorely." "Be firm, young man," was the reply, "and you'll get your reward in Heaven." A few weeks later the lad complained again. "Mr. Diamond," he said, "I don't know what to do. This time it's that beautiful redhead who is pursuing me." "Resist, my son, and you will get your reward in Heaven." "I don't know how much longer I can resist," the young man said. "By the way, Mr. Diamond, what do you think this reward will be that I will get in Heaven?" The answer came quickly, "A bale of hay, you jackass!"

"Oh pardon me. I thought it was the bedpost."

COLLOQUIAL A mountaineer girl and her hillbilly boyfriend had just been married, and, since no formal honeymoon was planned, they moved directly into the hillbilly's cabin right after the ceremony.

That night, a friend who had been unable to attend the wedding, went to the cabin to offer his congratulations. Answering his knock on the door was the bride, all dressed up in her new 'store-bought' clothes. She accepted his congratulations and then remarked that she and her spouse were about to go to bed.

"But you're dressed," stammered the friend, "You folks goin' to bed with all your clothes on?"

"Wal," smiled the country gal, "Newt said we'd be agoin' to town 'bout eleven o'clock tonight, so I can't see the need fer undressin'!"

JOLLY JOKER In the morning was pretty Dolly
Moaning her nocturnal folly.
He had looked like a funny old bloke,
And she had thought him just a joke,
But the joke was on Dolly, by golly!

BARE FACTS The census taker was considerably surprised when the mistress of the house opened the door and displayed her matronly self in a state of nudism.

"Please don't be shocked," she said. "I'm a nudist."

So, fortified by a college education which had prepared him for life, he asked the routine questions.

"And how many children do you have, Ma'am?" he asked, trying not to look at her and write at the same time.

"Twenty," she answered.

"My," he said, "you're not a nudist, lady. You just don't have time to get dressed."

A BULL'S EYE Elsie, the glamour cow, had been turned out to vacation in a lush pasture of emerald green. One side of the pasture she discovered to be fenced with barbed wire — a fence a full eight feet tall. And on the other side of the fence was quite the handsomest bull Elsie had ever seen.

Elsie and the bull started a flirtation in the coyest bovine fashion. "You must come over and see me some time," invited Elsie, "if you think you can jump that fence." And she flicked her tail and walked away. Taunted by the invitation, the bull went hastily to the other side of his pen. Lowering his head he took a long run and when he reached the fence, he took a very high jump. He alighted in the pasture with Elsie.

Elsie ran over to where he was. "Oh, I know you," she exclaimed. "You're Ferdinand, the bull."

"Just call me Ferdie," said the bull, "that damned fence was higher than I thought it was."

TICKLISH A wild goose is one that is an inch off centre.

NO, NO, LINDA This busy executive decided to take up golf as a diversion and one day brought a couple of golf balls into the office. His secretary Linda, who was not the outdoor type had never seen these before and asked her boss what they were. "Why, golf balls of course," he answered. During the following week, he was on the links again and came into the office with another couple of golf balls which he placed on his desk. This time Linda wasn't going to show her ignorance, so she remarked knowingly, "Oh, Mr. Seymour, I see you've shot another golf."

BEST MAN Then there was the one about those two close pals, Pedro and Pancho. It seems that Pedro was getting married. So they had the usual beeg wedding feast, with much wine. Things were going fine, until Pedro missed his beautiful bride. Upon closer examination of the group, he found his pal, Pancho, was also among the missing. Naturally Pedro started searching the premises. Upon looking into the bridal chamber, he closed the door softly, and crept softly down the stairs to his guests, saying excitedly, "Queek, Queek, Everybody, come look . . . Pancho are so drunk, he theenk he are me."

SAD, BUT TRUE The young couple came into the dining room on the fifth day of their honeymoon. The waiter approached them for their order.

"You know what I like, honey, don't you?" queried the bride.

"Yes, I know," stammered the husband, "but we have to eat sometime."

HO-HUM "The Captain is very nice," said the lady in the steamer-chair to her fellow-passenger, "but very boring."

"Yes?" prompted her companion. "And how do you find the Purser?"

"Quite all right — oh quite," continued the first lady, "but boring."

"And the Chief Steward?"

"A likable chap — but so, SO boring."

"Dear!" exclaimed the other, "You've certainly been bored this passage."

"Yes," she sighed, "How're you doin'?"

"And I say to *hell* with ADLER."

FOWL PLAY A girl of our acquaintance was shopping in her neighborhood market and found herself behind an austere dame at the meat counter. This member of the local elite requested with much dignity that the butcher make some suggestion for her dinner menu. "Of course," said the butcher, "how about a nice ox tongue, to be served with spinach?"

"What?" exclaimed the haughty one. "Do you have the nerve to suggest that I eat anything that has been in a cow's mouth?"

"Well, Madam," came back the butcher, "I noticed that you included eggs in your order this morning."

IMPOLITE Mae: "Oh what a cute little baby; red-headed, too. Was his father red-headed?"

Gae: "I don't know. He didn't take his hat off."

BLOOEY Harold Jonsen, not feeling quite up to the mark, asked his druggist for a prescription. The druggist prepared a small box of pills and handed these to Harold with the remark: "Take these."

Harold came in the next day and said he felt no better.

The druggist asked, "Did you take those pills?"

"Yes, I swallowed it."

"Swallowed what?" asked the druggist.

"The box," said Harold.

"You swallowed box and all?" asked the amazed druggist.

"Sure," said Harold. "Didn't you tell me to?"

The druggist leaned over the counter shaking his finger. "You just wait," he said, "until the lid comes off that box!"

SIDE TRACKED A farmer munching on a cookie was watching a big rooster chasing a hen and gaining ground at every lap. The farmer threw a piece of cookie in front of the racing pair. The rooster came to a sliding stop and gobbled up the tidbit.

"Gosh," said the farmer, "I hope I never get that hungry."

SMART TART The owner of a big furniture store went to New York to buy some stock and met a really beautiful girl in the hotel elevator. But she was French and they couldn't understand a word of each other's language.

So he took out a pencil and notebook and drew a sketch of a taxi. She nodded her head and laughed and they went for a ride in the park.

Then he drew a picture of a table in a restaurant with a question mark and she nodded, so they went to dinner.

After dinner he sketched two dancers and she was delighted. They went to a night club and danced and had a lovely evening.

At length she motioned for the pencil and drew a picture of a four-poster bed.

He was dumbfounded. He's never been able to figure out how she knew he was in the furniture business.

THE OTHER CHEEK Father and daughter on a shopping tour were in a crowded department store elevator. A stout woman gave this gentleman an outraged look and smacked him squarely in the face. He compressed his lips and said nothing. As they emerged on the ground floor, his daughter said, "I hated that woman too, papa. She stepped on my foot, so I pinched her right on the heine!"

"You sonofabitch!"

SHE KNOWS A mixed group was discussing beauty and women. "I think the most fascinating thing about a woman is her lips," said one man.

"I don't agree," said another: "I think it's her hair."

"Not at all," said a third, "It's her eyes."

A lady in the party sniffed, elevated her nose sharply and said, "I'm going to get out of here before one of you boys tells the truth."

BLIND ARTICLE This is a story about a honeymoon couple.

The bridegroom, who, all too late, was remembering his friend's warning against committing the fatal error, gazed ruefully at the scorched toast, the messy looking fried egg, the blackened bacon, and the anemic-looking coffee placed before him. "Hell, you can't cook, either!" he raged.

LEATHER-NECKERS A Marine regiment was sent back for rest after a rough tour of duty at the front. At the base they discovered a contingent of Wacs billeted and awaiting assignments to various posts. The Marine colonel addressed himself to the Wac commander, warning her that his men had been in the front lines a long time and might not be too careful about their attitudes toward the Wacs.

"Keep 'em locked up," he told the Wac commander, if you don't want any trouble."

"Trouble?" said she. "There'll be no trouble. My girls have it up here," and she tapped her forehead significantly.

"Madam," barked the Marine, "it makes no difference where they have it, my boys will find it. Keep 'em locked up."

GORGEOUS GEORGE

"Noisy" George was a salesman in the N. Y. Garment District but he heard so much about fabulous commissions made in insurance that he decided to get into that racket. Accordingly, he presented himself to the manager of an insurance office saying, "My friend, this is your lucky day. Noisy George is ready to work for you." The manager asked if he had any experience and George answered, "No, but I don't need it. I can sell anything. Just test me, brother." The man behind the desk said, "O.K. Hot Shot. Here is a policy for $100,000. I want you to sell it to the president of the Brown and Ohio Railroad, and don't come back until you do."

The very next day, George barged into the insurance office and plunked the policy on the manager's desk, signed and sealed. The man looked at it in amazement but the happy look on his face soon changed into a frown. "What's wrong?" said George. To which the manager retorted, "Where's the specimen?" "What specimen?" cried George, "you didn't tell me anything about a damn specimen." He reached out his hand, "All right, let's have the bottle!"

The following day, George came into the office carrying two buckets, one in each hand; and the buckets were far from empty. He kicked open the door to the manager's office and stood there holding the buckets. The insurance man, not knowing what to expect next from this character, said, "Well, let's have it. What's the gag?"

"It's no gag, boss," answered George. "I went back for the specimen like you told me, but when I busted in on the president he was holding a meeting of the board of directors, so I sold them a group plan!"

HOLD EVERYTHING

An armless man walked up to the bar. "Give me a beer," he said.

"Sure!" said the bartender as he sold the foamy stein to the thirsty one.

"Sorry," said the customer, "but I have no arms. Wonder if you'd be so kind as to hold it up while I drink?"

"You bet I will," said the bartender — and he did.

"Now," said the armless one, "I wonder if you will please get in my hip pocket and get my handkerchief — then wipe the foam from my lips?" And again the accommodating bartender complied.

"And here, in my left-hand pocket you'll find the change to pay for the drink," said the unfortunate customer.

The bartender got his money, rang up the sale and turned again to the armless one, who forthwith started a conversation.

"It's tough," he said, "to be like this. It causes me no end of embarrassment to be always having to ask people to do things for me. And, by the way, where is your rest room?"

"Four blocks north and two east," snorted the excited bartender.

SLIGHT ERROR

There was a time Jeremiah went up to his aged Grandfather and said, "Grandpappy, you're getting pretty old and feeble. Don't you think you'd better go to the poor house?"

"You're dadburned right, sonny. I'm a rarin'. Let's get going."

"Okay, Grandpappy, but I can't understand why you're so anxious to go to the poor house."

"Poor house? POOR HOUSE! Ye gads . . . my mistake, Bub!"

"But lady, how else can I measure your slacks?"

OH, THE PITY OF IT ALL

A young man of about twenty-one came home one day with a big smile on his face. "Father," he said, "I am in love with the most wonderful, the most beautiful, the most— Dad, I'm going to get married."

"Who is the girl?" asked Dad.

"The girl? Why she is the most marvel—"

"Never mind showing off those adjectives you learned at college and tell me her name," said Pop quite vexed.

"Her name is Lily Diamond, and she is as pure as—"

"Lily Diamond," exclaimed the pater. "My God, this is terrible. My son, you can't marry that girl!"

"What do you mean, I can't marry Lily?"

"Listen my son, and you shall hear the sad story I have to tell you. You can't marry that girl because she's your half-sister. Take it like a man, my boy, and remember there are certain things a gentleman never repeats," and with this the old man left his son, crying alone in the room. The boy's mother walked in and upon seeing him crying, pried the entire story out of him.

"You have nothing to cry about," she said as she was trying to control herself from having another hysterical fit of laughter, "He ain't even your father."

RSVP

A cat was seen running wildly down alleys, up fire escapes, down cellars and what not. A neighbor knew whose cat it was and reported it. "Your cat is running around like mad." "I know," came the reply. "He's just been sterilized and he's rushing around cancelling engagements."

EYES HAVE IT

"One thing I have learned in my long experience with the fair sex," said the sly looking one to his drinking companion, "is that you can't trust a woman with brown eyes!"

"Zounds!" exclaimed the other, "I've been married for two years and it occurs to me that I don't know what color eyes my wife has."

He bolted from the bar and whipped home. His wife was in bed asleep. Creeping closer he lifted her eyelid.

"Brown, by God!" he roared.

Brown crawled out from under the bed and said, "How the devil did you know I was under here?"

FIRST COME

"Mama, come out and swing me," said a 5 year old. The harassed Mother replied she was busy.

A few minutes later the tot again reminded, "Mama you said you would swing me."

The Mother, getting provoked, said, "Mary Jane, I can't now I have to nurse the baby first."

"Oh, he can wait," replied Mary Jane, "you haven't got him plugged in yet!"

SOUNDS FISHY

The professor of biology was explaining to his class the spawning of fish. "So you see," he concluded, "the female fish deposits her eggs, the male fish comes along and fertilizes them, and then later the little fish are hatched." One of the girls held up her hand. "You mean, Professor, that the father and mother fish—that they—that before that nothing happens?"

"Nothing," said the professor, "which doubtless explains the expression, 'Poor Fish'!"

59

MONKEY BUSINESS

A lady who lives in a small Minnesota town had two pet monkeys. Very fond of them, too. One day one of them took sick and died.. A couple of days later the other one died of a broken heart. Wishing to keep them, the kindly lady took them to an animal stuffer. The man asked her if she wanted them mounted.

"Oh, no," she replied, "just have them holding hands."

HOT OFF THE WIRE

A traveling man, suddenly deciding to spend a week-end at home, boarded a train and sent the customary wire to his wife. Upon his arrival he found her in the loving embraces of a boy friend. Angrily he left the house, took a room in a hotel, and applied next day for a divorce. The father-in-law, hearing of the affair, called the young man and sought to placate him in behalf of his daughter.

"Rose has always been a good wife to you, Henry," explained the old man. "If she has made a misstep there is probably an explanation for it."

"It's no use," replied Henry, "I'm going to proceed with the divorce."

"Then meet me at lunch tomorrow and we'll talk it over. In the meantime I'll see Rose again."

"All right," said Henry, "I'll meet you but I'm through."

At noon next day the two met at a restaurant.

"Henry, old boy," exclaimed the older man, slapping his son-in-law on the back. "Everything is okay. I knew Rose had a good reason for that little episode."

"Oh, yeah," said Henry.

"Sure," beamed the old man. "She didn't get your telegram."

SPLASH Mrs. Up-to-date was noted for all the new-fangled gadgets and appliances she had installed into her home. Her newest one was a musical toilet seat; when one sat on it the soft strains of a beautiful melody filled the room. The repertoire was wide and varied. One never knew what to expect, whether it would be a ballad or a classic, a march or boogie-woogie.

Three of the women in the neighborhood had heard about the gadget and decided to call in order to see it for themselves. No sooner were they seated when one of them expressed a desire to use the bathroom. "How was it?" asked the others curiously.

"Honestly," she marveled, "I can't get over it; it's amazing. I no sooner sat down when seemingly out of nowhere came the beautiful melody of Shubert's Serenade."

The second woman hurried to see it; she too, was amazed. "It played 'Tale of Vienna Woods,' by Strauss. It was simply wonderful," she said.

The third woman was now anxious to see it. The others waited for her to return; time passed, and they became worried, and finally they went to see what was keeping her so long. Upon opening the door they found her busy mopping.

"What happened?" they chorused.

"That damn thing!" the woman said indignantly as she pointed to the toilet, "I no sooner got seated than it started playing 'The Star Spangled Banner'."

IT'S A SHAM Clerk (to young lady): "Awfully sorry ma'am, but this two dollar bill is counterfeit."

Young lady: "Dammit, I've been seduced."

 HEY!

UNDERCOVER

Two partners in the garment center were quite successful, when suddenly, out of a clear sky, ruin fell on them. One of them ran about the place, tearing the hair out of his head by the handful. The other seemed to be more calm about it. He strutted up and down, his hands in pockets.

"Bum!" yelled the first. "Louse! Look how you enjoy this trouble. I'm going around tearing the hair from my head and you walk around like a sport."

"Never mind," said the other partner. "I'm tearing my hair out too. But nobody sees me."

KINSEY WAS HERE

The elderly and dignified gentleman standing at the bus-stop was annoyed with the inebriated bum who was pestering him.

"Thash a very purty ring ya got, pal," observed the souse. "Whersh ya get it?"

The man shrugged and replied tartly, "My fairy godmother gave it to me."

"Yer what?"

"My fairy godmother!" he repeated. "Haven't you a fairy godmother?"

The drunk pondered a moment, then said, "Nope! But I got an uncle we're not so sure of!"

RULES IS RULES

A Union organizer went to a bawdy house and he appraisingly looked over the girls. "There," he said to the matron, "I'll take that one," he pointed to a cute little blonde number.

"Oh, no you don't," said the matron. "You'll take that one over there," and she pointed to an old haggard looking girl who sat alone in a corner. "She's got seniority rights."

"Now here's something I can
get my teeth into!"

JACKPOT QUESTION   A man reading the morning newspaper while seated at breakfast with his wife and child, suddenly shouted, "Oh, my goodness! Here's an article saying the clergyman who married us was never properly ordained and is an impostor! Do you realize what this means? We were never legally married! Oh, my! What will the people at the office say? What will the boys at the club think? Oh, what will I do?"

"What will you do?" shrieked his wife, "What about me? How can I face my friends? What will my neighbors say behind my back?"

At this point, Junior spoke up, "Never mind about you two! How about *me*?"

OH YEAH   The origin of the saying "Oh yeah" has been attributed to the bridegroom who, upon hearing his bride say, "Now I lay me down to sleep," said to himself, "Oh yeah!"

NO ICE TODAY   Wrapped in a bath towel, a neighbor of mine was answering the telephone in the kitchen. As she hung up she heard heavy footsteps in the back hall, and saw the door knob turning. Thinking it must be the ice man, she ducked quickly into the broom closet. Just as she was breathing a sigh of relief, the door opened: and she was confronted by a very surprised young man! Horrified, she pulled her towel tight around her embarrassment, remembering that the gas meter was in the closet.

After a nightmarish pause, she blurted out in desperation, "Oh, I thought you were the ice man!"

The meter reader's eye widened. Then he smiled, tipped his hat and murmured, "Lucky man!"

BUTTON, UTTON, HERE COMES MOTHER

Here's a scene that took place on a crowded trolley car. A young lady is vainly groping for her purse to pay her fare. A young man is standing nearby with anguish written plainly on his handsome features.

Young man: "Pardon me, Miss, but may I pay your fare?"

Young Lady: "Sir!"

Y. M.: "I beg your pardon again, young lady, but won't you let me pay your fare?"

Y. L.: "Why, I don't even know you and anyway I'll have this purse open in a minute."

Continued groping.

Y. M.: "I really must insist on paying your fare. You've unbuttoned my pants three times."

INFERIORITY COMPLEX

The newlyweds had been married the day before and this was their first breakfast together. Shyly, the bride spoke. "Darling, I have a confession to make. I should have told you before. I suffer from asthma."

"Thank Heavens," cried the groom, "and all the time I thought you were hissing me."

HOLD ON!

A new and proud daddy, dashed to the hospital to visit his family. At the door to his wife's room, he met a cute little nurse carrying a cute little baby. The nurse held the child forward for the father's inspection. The beaming papa held the baby, looked at the nurse, and said, "Isn't little Arthur a handsome devil?"

The nurse replied, "Oh, this one isn't yours. This child's name is Alice and please let go of my finger."

GOOD QUERY, DEARIE

A group of men were in the club before dinner. The talk, for no good reason turned to married life.

"Well," said one fellow, "the real comfort in life comes when you are settled down with one woman you love. You can argue all you want, but it's my opinion that, once they've settled down, most men remain faithful."

Most of the men agreed with him, but an older man in the group shook his head. "I don't agree at all," he asserted. "And if you fellows are honest, you'll know I am right. I'll bet any and all of you men a new hat there isn't one of you who hasn't strayed from the straight and narrow since he's married."

"I'll take that bet," cried one, swiftly.

"How long have you been married?" asked the cynic.

"Since last Saturday," was the reply.

The crowd roared, of course — and one of the listeners was so amused that he could hardly wait to get home and tell his wife about it. At the end of the story he laughed and laughed. But his laughter died as he noticed a strange expression on his wife's face. "Don't you think the story very funny?"

"Very funny," she replied quietly, "But where is your new hat?"

SECOND HAND

"Yes, ma'm, what can I do for you?" asked the salesgirl.

"I'm going to be married next Tuesday and I would like to get some silk pajamas. What colors are appropriate for a bride?"

"White is the preferred color if it is your first marriage, and lavender if you have been married before."

"Well, you'd better give me some white ones with just a wee touch of lavender in them."

"Go ahead! Everyone else does."

HANDS OFF A new waiter at the Colony Club served a woman in extreme decollete. As she stooped to recover her napkin, a part of her anatomy popped out. The waiter adroitly put it back for her.

The captain noted this and called the waiter over. "Francois, where did you work before you came here?" he asked.

"Oh, at the Marquery, the Ambassador, at Pierre's — you know where I worked — you have my references."

"Did you do that sort of thing where you worked before?" asked the Captain.

 Certainly, when necessary," said Francois.

"Well, you are now working at the Colony Club. Hereafter when this occurs, please use two warm spoons."

OH Oh, George, let's not park here
Oh, George, let's not park
Oh, George, let's not
Oh, George, let's
Oh, George
Oh

WHAM Grandpappy: "Doc, you remember that 'vitality' medicine you gave me last week?"

Doctor: "Yes. What about it?"

Grandpappy: "I accidentally dropped it in the well."

Doctor: "Goodness, man! You're not drinking the water, are you?"

Grandpappy: "Heck, no! We can't even get the pump handle down."

FOUND WEEK END

This "casanova" recently took a girl to a big store on Friday afternoon to buy her a fur coat. He insisted on the finest. A $5,000 fox wasn't good enough. Up and up the price went until it stopped at a $20,000 mink. The girl almost swooned over his devotion, and naturally grew very loving.

He then told the salesman, "I'm sure you want to check my credit. As it's too late now, I suggest you do it Monday morning and then I'll pick up the coat."

On Monday morning, the store checked and found the guy's credit couldn't be worse. Just then Lover Boy himself, walked in. As the salesman started to tell him his credit was worthless, he smiled and said, "Yes, I know. I just dropped in to thank you for a wonderful weekend."

RICE CONTROL

He: "Would you commit adultery for a million dollars?"
She: "Why, yes, I think I would."
He: "Would you commit adultery for two dollars?"
She: (shocked) "Oh, what do you think I am?"
He: "We've settled that. What we are haggling about now is the price."

LAY THAT PISTOL DOWN

A husband came home one night and found his wife entertaining a strange man. He was about to shoot the man when his wife cried, "Don't, don't! Who do you think gave us that house in the country, and that handsome Packard roadster and my mink coat?" "Is this the man?" asked her husband. His wife nodded violently. The pistol hand dropped. "Wrap him up in a blanket . . . he might catch cold."

71

THE MIRACLE
A hermit once lived in a hut on a hill
No legend or myth is this tale that I tell
For my grandfather said that he knew him quite well
this hermit
He lived all alone by the shores of a lake
Concoctions of herbs for his health he would make
And nothing but fish would the good man partake
on Fridays
Now to the inquisitive public his portals he closed
Once a year he'd bathe both his body and clothes
How the lake ever stood it a fish only knows,
and he won't tell.
But one morning he rose all dripping and wet,
And his horrified vision two fair maidens met;
Now at the feminine business he was not a vet.
So he blushed.
He picked up his hat which lay on the beach
To cover as much as it's broad rim could reach
And he yelled to the girls in a horrified screech
"Go way now."
But the girls just laughed at his terrible plight
Begged the hermit to show them the wonderful sight;
But he clung to his hat with all of his might
To hide it.
When just at that minute a villainous gnat
Made the hermit forgetful of where he was at;
So he let go the hat and struck at the Gnat
Oh, Horrors.
And now I have come to the thread of the tale,
The hermit turned red and then he turned pale;
He uttered a prayer, for prayers never fail,
So 'tis said.
Of the truth of the story there's no doubt at all
Some angel heard and answered his call,
Tho' he let go the hat, the hat did not fall,
Miracle.

"Well how'd you make out with the old man?"

OUT OF PLACE

My wife and I were shopping, and having lunch in the exquisite Coral Room in the super-duper, swank new Bullocks Pasadena, "Most beautiful store in the world."

Excusing myself to go to the men's room, I asked directions from the third floor level floor walker.

"Proceed through the hand carved arch on your left," explained the suave gentleman in the striped pants, "descend to the left to the second floor level, pass through the gallery of the Italian Renaissance Period, thence through the Peacock Court of Royal Persian Rugs, Draperies and Antiques, and just beyond you will find the accommodations you seek."

I was gone for what my wife considered a terribly long time, and upon my return she demanded to know where I had been, what I had been doing, and what took me so long.

"I've been to the men's room," I answered. "I proceeded through the hand carved arch on your left, descended to the second level, wended my way through the Art Gallery of Italian Renaissance Period, and found the ultra ornate accommodations of the men's room. But upon self examination — it looked so shabby, that I took it across the street to the gasoline station."

MIRACLE ON 34TH STREET

The bus driver charged a lady full fare (ten cents) for her son, who had on long pants.

At the next corner a small boy wearing short trousers paid only five cents (half fare).

At the next stop, a lady mounted the bus and the driver didn't charge her anything. Why? . . .

Don't have an evil mind — the lady had a transfer.

"I've told you a thousand times not to
use mama's side!"

CONFESSION GOOD FOR THIS HEEL

"I've made love to so many women," he confided, "I think it's time I changed. Tonight I'm going home to my wife and confess and ask her forgiveness."

Of course his wife was hurt by his confession and she asked, "Was it that little dancer, Anita?"

"I'm sorry," he replied gallantly, "I won't say."

His wife continued, "I bet it was that model, Patricia."

He kept his silence.

"I know who it is . . . it's that hat-check girl in the theater."

"Sorry, I can't tell you."

"All right," said his angry spouse, "if you won't tell me who it was, I won't forgive you."

Next day: "Did your wife forgive you?"

"No," was the reply, "but she gave me three swell leads."

ALOHA

Then there was the fellow who entered a restaurant and ordered baked beans covered with pineapple juice. His wife liked Hawaiian music.

KNOTTED

The bride speaks from the luxurious depths of an oversized bed. "Darling, I can hardly believe we're married." At the opposite end of the room the crouched figure of the groom mutters something. Seconds tick by — again, "Darling, I can hardly believe we're married at last." No answer. More time drags by. Restlessly the bride speaks again. "Oh, honey, I can't believe we're really married."

The groom finally speaks, in a voice contorted with rage, "If I can get this damn shoelace untied you will."

"That's what it's called, and
no cheap cracks."

EGGHEAD   A fellow we call Egghead enticed me into a bar where he proceeded to get himself a snootful. I urged him to leave but he wished to avail himself of the wash room first so I waited patiently outside the door. He took so much time I was worried because I knew he was in sad shape. Suddenly, I heard a shriek and dashed into the lavatory to find him seated with a painful expression on his face. "Egghead," I said, "what the hell is the matter?" "I don't know," he whined, "I pulled this lever and almost ruined myself."

"No wonder, you darn fool," I answered, "you're sitting on the mop bucket."

SWISH   Two of "the boys" were enjoying a vacation in New York. As they strode up and down the big city's thoroughfares their high tenor voices and their queer mannerisms caused many to turn and look — and laugh.

One day they were out for a walk and were crossing Brooklyn Bridge. As they approached the middle one of them said to the other, "Oh, just look at those great big boats. Aren't they just simply beautiful, Dearie?"

"Oh, they sure are," replied the other, "and such great big things."

"Lookie over there!" exclaimed the first one, "that one's different from all the rest. I wonder what ever kind of a boat that can be?"

"You big silly," explained the second, "that's a ferry boat."

"Oh, mercy," said the first, "I didn't know we had a Navy!"

MALL WORLD The young man made a rather hasty purchase at a drug store and answered the druggist's knowing smile with a short and glowing description of the date he had that night.

That evening the young man rang the bell and was invited into the girl's home and introduced to her parents. A general discussion of the weather and other equally important subjects was carried on for some time before the young man said, "It's about time for us to be getting started if we are going to the church. Won't you come with us?" he asked the parents.

The girl's parents refused at first, but the young man was so insistent that they finally agreed and the four of them went to church together.

About half way through the service the girl leaned over to the young man. "I didn't know you were so religious," she whispered.

"No," the young man replied, "No, and I didn't know your old man was a druggist either."

FOR SURE The difference between war and peace is there never has been a good war.

ONCE An American meets an elderly Britisher in a sporting club.

A: "Care for a game of checkers?"

B: "No. Tried it once, didn't like it."

A: "Care for a game of chess?"

B: "No. Tried it once, didn't like it."

A: "Care for a game of tennis?"

B: "No, but my son will play tennis with you."

A: "Your only child, I presume."

STUNNED A certain young lady was invited up to her boy friend's apartment the other evening to look at his etchings. When they arrived at his apartment, she was surprised to find no etchings at all. In fact, to her amazement, she discovered he had no chairs, no tables, no furniture, at all. She was floored.

HE'LL NEVER BE QUEEN A king, who had three daughters for marriage, made the statement that any prince in the kingdom who could pass certain tests could marry his choice of the three. One of the daughters was a blonde, one a brunette, and one a red-head. All the princes in the kingdom tried to pass the tests and failed. One day Prince Charming came up on his white charger and said to the king, "I understand you have three daughters for marriage."
And the king said, "Yes, if you pass certain tests."
So the king explained the tests to him and Prince Charming went forth into the world. A year later, he came back and told the king of all the dragons he had slain, of all the fair maidens he had rescued, and of all the battles he had fought.
The king said, "Son, you may have your choice of my daughters for marriage. Which do you choose?"
He chose the king because this is really a fairy tale.

BUENO A young steno had just returned from a summer vacation trip through old Mexico. She was excitedly telling her friends all about it. "Did you learn much Spanish while you were there?" one of the girls asked.
"Oh, yes," she replied, "I found out that Manana means tomorrow and that pajama means tonight."

When the lights go on again, all over the world.

HANDYMAN A big Kansas farmer found it necessary to go to Minneapolis for several months and decided to leave one of his best workers in charge. "I want you to take care of things, Hank, as if I were here myself. Understand?" Hank nodded.

Four months later the boss farmer returned to find everything in shape. Said Hank, pointing things out, "the chicks have been laying plenty of eggs, the wheat has grown double strong, the vegetables are better than they've ever been, and as for those monthly spells your daughter used to have, I've even got those stopped."

FOR MEN ONLY? A luscious blonde got a job distributing free sticks of gum, by way of advertisement, on street corners. One evening after work she ran into an old friend. "Say, I hear you're planning to get married," said the friend. "When's the big event going to come off?"

"In a few months," the blonde replied.

"That's fine! And what are you doing in the mean while?"

"Oh," responded the luscious one, pursing her lips prettily, "I'm giving away samples."

BUSY MRS. B Boris who comes from Czechoslovakia has been in this country only a few months. He does not speak English very well, and in conversation one day was asked, "Boris, what is it that you are most anxious to see in America?"

"Well," replied Boris, "I weesh most to meet dat famous Mrs. Beech who have so many sons in last war."

THAT OLD FEELING — Then there's the case of the sweet young thing who decided she'd rather be a young man's slave than an old man's darling, with the explanation that she hated the thought of feeling old age creeping up on her.

AN OLD PRO — During a recent Vice Crusade in New York three gold diggers were arrested. They were all squawking about their innocence, but it had very little effect. The Judge finally silenced them and got down to the business of the day. He looked at the first girl, and she rolled her eyes and exhibited her legs. "What's your business?" the Judge demanded.

"Oh, my business!" she cooed, "I'm a dressmaker and this awful cop—"

"Thirty days," interrupted His Honor.

The second girl was called and she tried the weeping stunt.

"Oh, your Honor, I'm a respectable dressmaker with a family to support, a crippled mother and a dying baby—"

"Thirty days," rasped the Judge.

He didn't waste much time on the third. She was called to order and the Judge asked, "What's your business?"

"I'm a whore," she answered.

The Judge looked relieved. "How's business?" he asked.

"Just lousy," she said, "what with all those dressmakers around."

CHANCES FOR ADVANCES — The sudden entrance of a wife has caused many a secretary to change her position.

FLYING LOW

A young lady went to a dance, and she had a low-cut, strapless gown on, and around her neck she wore a little golden airplane on a long chain. All night she noticed a young man, staring at her. So in her embarrassment, she held up the airplane and said, "Oh you like my airplane, huh?" The young man smiled and said, "No ma'am, I was just admiring the landing field."

FLASHBACK

Ole Swenson was taken to a hospital with a broken leg. "How did it happen?" asked the nurse as she came to sit beside his bed to take the case history.

"Well," he began, "It was twenty years ago and—"

"I don't want to know what happened twenty years ago," she said impatiently, "what happened now?" Each time, however, he began the same way and finally in desperation she had to let him have his way.

"I went to work for a farmer twenty years ago," he explained, "and the first night after I went to bed, the farmer's beautiful daughter came into my room and asked if I wanted anything. I said, 'No.' The second night she came again, and this time she was clad in her nightgown. Again she asked if I wanted anything and again I told her 'No.' The third night when she came in she was almost entirely nude. I could see every curve plainly as the moonlight streamed in the window. 'Do you want anything?' she inquired warmly. 'No thanks,' I said. 'I have had a good supper, the bed is comfortable and I feel fine.'

I wondered at the time what she thought I could possibly want? Then yesterday, as I was shingling the roof, it came to me like a flash."

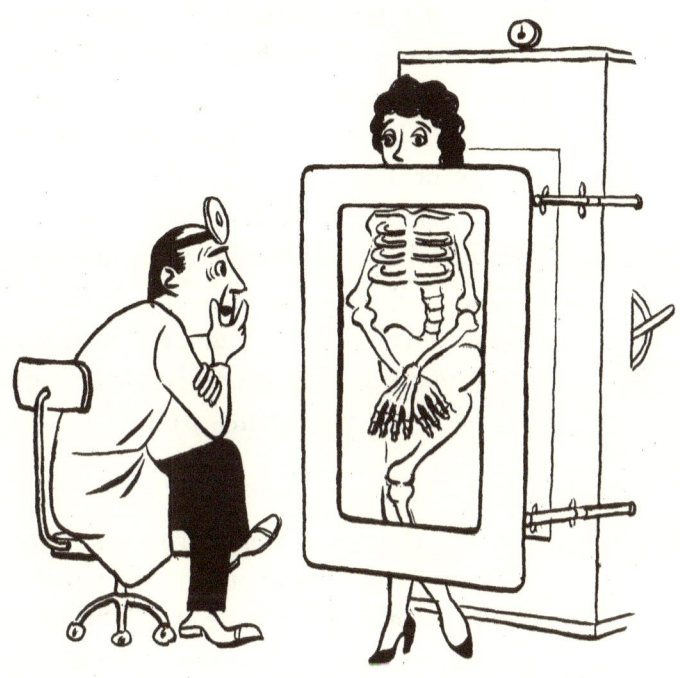

TALE WITH A MORAL — Travelers to Salt Lake City frequently ask the natives about the Mormon practice of polygamy. Although the practice was abolished many years ago, they generally relate a fable they themselves used to enjoy rather than disappoint visitors.

This Salt Lake Cityite told of his great grandfather who had anywhere from thirty-six to ninety-six wives. He had a bachelor apartment, to which he had a runner bring him, at the end of a day's work, and in rotation, five or six of his wives. As one wife left by a back door, the runner brought another in the front door.

The interested visitor interrupted, "Your great grandfather must have died rather early."

"Oh, no," said the native, grinning, "he died at eighty-seven. But the runner died at thirty-five."

And he adds, "The moral is: 'It isn't the lovin' that kills you, it's the runnin' after.' "

ALTAR-RATION — Private Haynes was back from his furlough and was telling his buddies about his girl friend. "Last night I finally got her to say yes." "Congratulations!" offered his buddies, "when is the wedding?"

"Wedding?" said Haynes, "What wedding?"

NAIVE — The little old lady was taking her first ocean voyage. A huge whale was sighted, and as the ship's passengers crowded the rails, sure enough the whale spouted—terrifically.

She gasped.

"It looks to me like it could at least quit laying on its back and showing off like that," she fumed as she sped toward her stateroom.

"I don't care who told you variety
is the spice of life."

Franklin On Marriage
A classic from American Letters

To my dear friend:

I know of no medicine fit to diminish the violent natural inclinations you mention; and if I did, I think I should not communicate it to you. Marriage is the proper remedy. It is the most natural State of Man, and therefore the State in which you are most likely to find solid Happiness. Your Reasons against entering into it at present appear to me not well founded. The circumstantial Advantages you have in view by postponing it, are not only uncertain, but they are small in comparison with that of the Thing itself, the being married and settled. It is the Man and Woman united that make the compleat human Being. Separate, She wants his Force of Body and Strength of Reason; he, her Softness, Sensibility, and acute Discernment. Together they are more likely to succeed in the World. A single man has not nearly the value he would have in the State of Union. He is an incomplete Animal. He resembles the odd half of a pair of Scissors. If you get a prudent, healthy Wife, your Industry in your Profession with her good Economy, will be a Fortune sufficient.

But if you will not take this Counsel and persist in thinking a Commerce with the Sex inevitable, then I repeat my former Advice, that in all your Amours you should prefer old Women to young ones.

You call this a Paradox and demand my Reasons. They are these:

1. Because they have more Knowledge of the World, and their Minds are better stored with Observations, their Conversation is more improving, and more lastingly agreeable.

2. Because when Women cease to be handsome they study to be good. To maintain their Influence over men, they supply the Diminution of Beauty by an Augmentation

of Utility. They learn to do a thousand Services small and great and are the most tender and useful of Friends when you are sick. Thus they continue amiable. And hence there is hardly such a thing to be found as an old Woman who is not a good Woman.

3. Because there is no Hazard of Children, which irregularly produced may be attended with much inconvenience.

4. Because through more Experience they are more prudent and discreet in conducting an Intrigue to prevent Suspicion. The Commerce with them is therefore safer with regard to your Reputation. And with regard to theirs, if the Affair should happen to be known, considerate People might be rather inclined to excuse an old Woman, who would kindly take care of a young man, form his Manners by her good counsels, and prevent his ruining his Health and Fortune among mercenary Prostitutes.

5. Because in every Animal that walks upright, the Deficiency of the fluids that fill the Muscles appears first in the highest Part. The face first grows lank and wrinkled; then the Neck; then the Breast and Arms; the lower parts continuing to the last as plump as ever: so that covering all above with a Basket, and regarding only what is below the Girdle, it is impossible of two Women to tell an old one from a young one. And as in the dark all Cats are grey, the Pleasure of Corporal Enjoyment with an old Woman is at least equal, and frequently superior every Knack being, by Practice, capable of Improvement.

6. Because the Sin is less. The debauching a Virgin may be her Ruin, and make her for Life unhappy.

7. Because the Compunction is less. The having made a young Girl miserable may give you frequent bitter Reflection; none of which can attend the making an old Woman happy.

8th and lastly. They are so grateful!

Thus much for my Paradox. But still I advise you to marry directly; being sincerely

Your affectionate friend,

BENJAMIN FRANKLIN

TURNABOUT

Two English gentlemen of the old school were discussing old acquaintances one evening in their London Club.

"What," asked one, "ever became of old Chumley?"

"Why didn't you hear? Chumley went to Africa on a game hunt, and by Jove, the chap took up with an ape!"

"An ape? Is the old boy queer?"

"No! It was a female ape!"

STOP IT ALREADY

A little boy went to school for the first time and the teacher explained that if he wanted to go to the washroom he should raise two fingers. The boy, looking puzzled, asked—"How's that going to stop it?"

PRIORITY

A gourmet of our acquaintance treated his family to a Sunday dinner out. He had called the restaurant the day before and ordered a special duck.

So, when our friend ushered his family into the dining room, he beamed with a sense of well-being and importance. The waitress brought in the duck —a choice viand obviously cooked to perfection, to judge from its luscious, golden brown appearance. But appearances were deceiving. The knife wouldn't cut it and the fork bent instead of puncturing it. In disgust, he called the waitress.

"Take this duck back and tell the chef where he can stick it."

She did as instructed and shortly returned.

"Pardon me, sir," she said, "there are two chickens and a steak ahead of you."

KILROY · WAS · HERE

BITTER CUP A golf tournament for ladies was staged by one of the swank Long Island country clubs. The day before the award of a trophy to the winner, the chairman of the committee discovered that no trophy had been bought. He hurried to the local jeweler, who informed him that he could not get the cup and have it engraved in 24 hours. He suggested that the sample cup he had on display be handed to the winner with the explanation that one just like it, with a suitable inscription, would be delivered to her sometime during the following week.

The next evening the winner of the tournament marched proudly up to the platform, to receive her trophy. The chairman, in the stress of the moment and with a few highballs under his belt, completely forgot to mention that the cup was merely a sample and one with the correct inscription would be delivered later to the winner. She took one look at the inscription on the cup and fainted dead away.

The chairman, more curious than courteous, picked up the cup and read the inscription before picking up the lady. And he felt like fainting too, when he read:

AWARDED TO THE
BEST WIRE-HAIRED BITCH
IN NASSAU COUNTY

DIAMOND EXCHANGE The sugar-daddy presented the beautiful chorus girl with a gorgeous diamond clip backstage.

"Oh, Mr. Gottrox! I'm going on in a minute. Can I wear it now?" she beamed.

"Certainly, my dear," he leered. "You may wear it until the end of the act."

WHAT'S A CAPON? It was just before dark, and the farmer went into his chicken house to separate the roosters from the pullets, so as to ready them for the market in the morning. Putting a temporary screen partition across the middle of the henhouse, eventually he had all the roosters plus a big capon on one side, and the pullets and hens on the other.

One enterprising hen found an opening she could just squeeze through into the rooster side of the partition. It was fun over there, but she knew her place. Next morning she sifted back through this opening into her own side of the chickenry. Immediately the other hens crowded excitedly around her, and one exclaimed:

"Say, it must have been wonderful to have been in there all night with all those young boys."

"Wonderful, nothing," griped the enterprising hen, "that big capon kept me in a corner all night long, and all he did was talk about his operation."

BOTTOMS UP Men make passes at girls that empty glasses.

SOUTHERN GENTLEMAN Mrs. Jones had been gone from her former home in Wynn, Ark., for seven years. She was now on her way back to attend a family reunion and was traveling by bus. After passing through Little Rock she fell asleep and upon awakening she didn't recognize any of the old landmarks. Thinking that she might have passed her destination, she asked the gentleman sharing the seat with her:

"Pardon me, but have I passed Wynn?"

"I didn't notice," replied the gentleman. "If you did, it was mighty ladylike."

WRONG PIECE A famous orchestra leader was sailing for Europe. His best friend was seeing him off. When about to leave for shore, he noticed that a very beautiful girl was occupying the cabin next to the musician.

"Lucky guy," commented the friend, "but she looks as if she would be hard to make."

"Don't you worry about that," boasted the musician, "I'll bet you five bucks that I get well acquainted with her before midnight."

"Oke, I'll take you up on that," agreed the friend, "but how am I going to know whether or not I win the bet?"

"Well, that's easy too," suggested the Lothario swing artist, "My program is being broadcast tonight. Listen in, and if you hear me play the piece, "I Love You Truly," you'll know you've lost the bet."

That night the friend listened to the program, but instead of the band playing, "I Love You Truly," he was amazed to hear "Red Sails in the Sunset!"

CAD I want a girl just like the girl Dad had on the side.

MEN IN WHITE Being confined in a hospital for a complete check-up, Joyce, a very shapely blonde was not surprised when a handsome chap dressed in white came in, pulled down the sheets and for some minutes looked her over. Shaking his head he left. Shortly he returned, pulled down the sheets and made another examination. The third time he came in, the blonde in desperation inquired, "Say, what in the world am I in here for, observation or examination?" The chap in white replied, "Darned if I know, lady, I'm just doing some painting out in the hall."

94

"Thank you James, that will be all for tonight."

AT LONG LAST   A new bride was asked what she had found to be the biggest thrill of marriage. "It was certainly thrilling when Henry took me to the license bureau. It was another thrill when the minister pronounced us man and wife. I got an awful bang out of seeing Henry sign the register 'Mr. and Mrs.' I do believe though, that my biggest thrill was thumbing my nose at the house detective."

FLOOR PLEASE   A young bridal couple went to a local hotel on their wedding night; the next morning the bride's closest girl friend telephoned her, to ask how married life agreed with her. "Oh, Marge," she replied. "I'm just awfully tired, dead tired. All night long it was up and down; in and out; up and down, in and out! Don't ever get a room next to an elevator!"

MOORE FUN   Bellhop: "Calling Mr. Moore. Calling Mr. Moore."
Clerk (not recognizing name): "Who is that being called?"
Bellhop: "I don't know. Some gal up in 213 keeps yelling for more."

CHARITY BEGINS AT HOME   A henpecked husband begged off one evening to go to a stag party. There would be only men there, he pleaded, so his wife needn't be jealous. But to his horror, when he arrived he found four naked women dancing. He called up his wife immediately. "Unintentionally, dearest, I told you a lie," he said. "I thought there would be only men here, but now naked girls are dancing about. What shall I do?" "If you think you can do anything, come right home," said his wife.

"Well don't do it again . . . *See*?"

VIRGIN TERRITORY

June (a bride) was showing her uncle over their new home.

"This is my room, uncle! You see we have twin beds, they are so much more hygienic. That's Harold's, this is mine."

Then uncle noticed a blue china clock on the mantel and remarked: "What a very charming clock."

"Yes," said June, "it's a wedding present from dear grandma."

A few weeks later uncle received a note from June telling how the blue clock had disappeared the very afternoon he was there; could he throw any light on it?

Uncle replied: "Dear June, look in Harold's bed."

JEALOUS

A rooster while strutting around the barnyard early one Easter Sunday morning came across a nest of brightly colored eggs. He cocked his head, thought a while — then made a beeline across the barnyard and knocked hell out of the peacock.

POWER OF SPEECH

He was the strong, silent type. When he walked into the cafe, ordered coffee and winked at the waitress, she smiled. "Want to go riding?" he asked. "Sure do. I'll be ready in five minutes."

So they got in the car and he drove out on the highway. Then he took off down a road. Then he drove down a lane. The lane came to a dead end and he stopped the car and cut the motor off.

Turning to her, he uttered his first speech. "Well, howaboutit?"

The waitress nodded and said, "Okay — you've out-talked me!"

"Now cough."

NO KIN DO   Zeke McCoy had just married Nellie Martin and off they went to a cabin in the mountains for a honeymoon. He had only been gone one day when he suddenly stormed into his pappy's cabin.

His pappy said, "Where's yore woman, son?"

Zeke countered, "I done shot her, paw!"

"What fer," said the old man.

"She were a virgin, Paw."

"Ya done right, son, if she weren't good nuff for her own folk, she ain't good nuff fer us!"

WELL HEELED   An American soldier goes into a London restaurant and sits down at a table. After a few moments a good looking filly jaunts over to his table and lays down the menu.

"What's good today?" he asks of the waitress.

"Rhubarb, rutabagas, ravioli, rice and roast," is her answer.

"Baby you sure do roll your r's."

"Yeah, maybe it's because of these high heels I'm wearing."

THE END HAS A CATCH   It was a marvelous spring evening. The grass had just turned an emerald green, the fruit trees were in bloom and the whole world seemed to have come to life again.

"What a beautiful day for a picnic," said one of the office gang, and it was one of those occasions when it was no sooner said than done. All the guys and gals got their heads together and it was only a matter of minutes until a weiner roast had been arranged for that evening.

(Next Page)

And so it was that at the appointed hour all of them were gathered at the favorite picnic grounds. What a happy lot they were as they gathered around the campfire. They giggled and laughed, told stories, sang and kidded each other endlessly. In due course of time, the golden sun sank behind the western horizon and the remaining embers of the camp fire faded lower and lower. And as darkness descended upon the universe, first one couple and then another left the happy circle to seek haven in the darkness that now surrounded them.

Seclusion!

One demure little miss was possessed of a very marked poetic streak. She and her boy friend left the circle of light and shrouded in darkness found themselves a place upon a little hillock. And there the sweet young thing commenced to emote.

"Isn't it marvelous out here tonight?" And then as if to answer her own question, she went on. "Here we are, all alone in a world of darkness. The golden sun has gone to rest and the earth now wears a mantle of black in mourning for a day that has passed. The tender south breeze blows ever so softly and carries upon its wings the delicate scent of the blossoms that bloom in the spring. The inky sky above is beautiful beyond words, with its millions of tiny stars that blink down at us so mysteriously. And just listen to the chirp of the myriad of crickets."

"All right, you dope," said her more mundane escort. "Wake up! Them ain't crickets — them's zippers!"

OT WEEK YET First Bride: "Does your husband snore in his sleep?" Second Bride: "I don't know, we've only been married three days."

WHAT DO Y'KNOW JOE

For some time, little Joe had been a confirmed thumb-sucker, and his mother was unsuccessful in breaking him of the habit. Finally, she said to him, "Joseph, if you continue to suck your thumb, your stomach will blow up bigger and bigger until it bursts."

This did the trick because it scared the lad.

A little while later, Joseph's mother was entertaining some guests at home, and among them was a lady who was very, very pregnant. Her frontal contour fascinated the boy who just stared at her. Not being able to control himself any longer, Joe pointed at her and (in a voice that everyone could hear) said, "I know what you've been doing!"

UNCOVERED

At Coney Island recently a bather found herself minus the top of her bathing suit when she came out of the surf. Stricken with embarrassment she crossed her arms in front of her chest and hurried across the beach. She almost made the bathhouse unnoticed when a small boy stood in her path and said, "Lady, if you are giving away those puppies, could I have the one with the pink nose?"

OH, WHAT HE SAID!

While visiting a dance at a school for the deaf and dumb a young man was fascinated as the speechless couples danced and gesticulated. An interpreter carefully explained what their fingers were saying. Suddenly the young man noticed two fellows over in the corner. One had his hand under his coat, moving his fingers wildly.

"What's he doing?" came the inquiry.

"Oh, him," was the explanation, "he's telling dirty stories!"

"Let's get married darling, we were made
for each other."

NOBLE GESTURE   In London, a certain lord married a woman forty years his junior.

The London Times' account of the ceremony stated that the bridgegroom's gift to the bride was an antique pendant.

CLOCK WATCHER   Exactly nine months after their wedding the Diamonds headed for the hospital, where Mrs. Diamond was rushed into the maternity ward. Mr. Diamond, like all good expectant fathers, paced the floor in the anteroom awaiting the joyous tidings. In due time the nurse put in her appearance. "Congratulations!" she said, "you're the father of a dandy seven-pound baby boy!"

"Fine!" exclaimed Diamond as he consulted his watch carefully for the time. "It's exactly nine o'-clock! Isn't nature grand?"

In a matter of minutes the nurse put in her appearance again. "What a lucky man you are," she said, "you have been twice blessed. Now you are also the father of a fine baby girl!"

"Great!" exclaimed Diamond, again consulting his watch carefully. "It is now exactly nine-thirty o'-clock. Isn't nature grand?" And with that remark he started off down the hall.

"Just a minute!" called the nurse. "Where are you going?"

"Oh, I just thought I'd go for a little stroll," explained Diamond. "The next one isn't due until ten forty-five!"

HELP   A young lady's definition of "like" and "love": "If I likes 'em I lets 'em but if I loves 'em I helps 'em."

READY-AIM   Greatly agitated, a young mother dashed into a drug store carrying her infant child. The druggist hurried to ascertain the cause of her distress.

"My baby swallowed a .22 calibre bullet!" she cried. "What shall I do?"

"Give it the contents of a castor oil bottle," replied the druggist calmly, "but don't point him at anyone."

HIS FUTURE   A representative for an insurance company that was
IS BEHIND   extending its business into foreign countries was trying to sell some insurance to a big fat eunuch, one of the Sultan's harem guards.

"I can sell you either accident insurance or a life policy," he told his prospective customer.

"Well," said the eunuch, "It's too late for an accident policy and—" he hesitated for a moment and then said, "I'm fixed for life."

OUP TO NUTS   At a mountaineer's cabin way up in the mountain a very large family were seated around the dinner table and as is customary there was no passing of food. When they wanted something they just stood up and reached for it and some of the reaches were pretty long. One of the older boys was sitting at the table and wanted a slice of bread, so he stood up and stretched far across the table for it. The father sitting at the side wrinkled his brow and said: "Maw, how old is Zeke now," and Maw said, "Nigh onto twenty I reckon Paw," and Paw very seriously said, "Maw it appears to me we better start putting pants on Zeke. Did you see what he dragged through the soup?"

82 YEARS YOUNG   Back home in East Texas, Old Man Jones confessed his troubles to the local doctor.

"It's sort of ticklish to talk about, Doc," he apologized. "But I need some vitamins or something, on account of when it comes to making love, I ain't got as much pep as I used to have."

"Well, that's natural," the Doc consoled. "How old are you?"

"Well, let's see. I'm a year older'n my wife, and she's 81. Guess I'm about 82 years old."

"And when did you first notice this lack of pep on your part?"

"Well, the first time was last night. That wasn't so bad, but be-doggone if we didn't notice it again this morning."

STATISTICS   A recent national poll was conducted for the sole purpose of determining why men get up in the middle of the night. Only 2.4%, it developed really have to get up. 1.6% go prowling around the kitchen to find something to eat.

The other 96% get up to go home.

RACY   Before the races Alexander took his girl around to the stables to look over the horses to see if they couldn't pick a winner. The first stall they looked into was that of a young stallion with a good record. The beast was in fine fettle, evidently, the way he was waving the distinguishing mark of his horsehood. Pearl considered it a while with sufficient interest. Then drawing her man away, she said, "Don't bet on him, Alec. Dat hoss dere ain't gonna win. He ain't got his mind on his business."

"The preliminaries are usually much better than the main bout . . . Don't you think?"

YOURS TRULY   The locale was a nudist colony. The boy and the girl were strolling through the woods. Shyly his words reached her blushing ears:

"Don't look now but I think I'm falling in love with you."

GOOD HUNTING   Into town on his regular Saturday visit came a lanky Tennessee mountaineer and his young wife. In the crook of his right arm nestled a week-old baby. The dry-goods merchant, who had not seen the couple in quite a long while, greeted then affably. "Come right in, folks, glad to see ye! Well, well, is that yore young 'un, Len?"

Len pondered thoughtfully for a moment, then replied, "Wal, yeah, I reckon it's mine. Leastaways, it wuz caught in my trap."

SPECIAL DUTY   A general, a colonel and a major were having a heated argument on the subject of sex. The general maintained that sex was 60 per cent work and 40 per cent fun. The colonel said it was 75 per cent work and 25 per cent fun. The major thought it was 90 per cent work and 10 per cent fun. At the height of the argument, a private appeared at the door. "Let's leave it to him," said the major.

The private listened carefully and said, with an air of absolute finality, "If you will pardon me, sirs, sex is 100 per cent fun and no work at all."

"How do you figure that?" cried the astonished officers.

"It is very simple," said the private. "If there was any work in it at all, you guys would have me doing it for you."

"I suppose you think *yours* don't!"

SOME PARTY   A young interne was making a morning visit in a maternity ward at a hospital. He stopped at the first bed and said:

"When do you expect your baby?"

"September 4."

He went on to the next bed and repeated his question.

"September 4," came the reply.

He went on to the next patient, and found her asleep. He turned to the occupant in the bed nearby, and said: "When does Mrs. —— expect her baby to be born?"

"I don't know," said this woman. "You see she didn't go on the picnic."

VICIOUS CYCLE   "He bought his girl a bicycle and now she peddles it all over town."

IT'S AN ILL WIND   The new stenographer seemed a terrible grouch. Nobody could ask her to do anything without getting a snappy comeback. She growled at this, grumbled at that; and made herself generally unpleasant. But since she proved a good worker, the boss let it go at that. One morning, however, she came in all smiles. She hummed to herself as she rattled the keys, and answered pleasantly when she was spoken to. Everybody was amazed. The boss gave her a lot of correspondence to answer. She did it in jig time, and laid the letters on his desk for him to sign. Mystified, he looked at her. "What's the matter, Mame?" he asked, "Are you sick?" She grinned back at him: "Am I sick? I'll tell the world I am!"

"I suppose everybody asks you the same question."

WHOA, NOW   Arriving home from an afternoon of shopping, Mrs. Jaxon discovered her husband in the act of packing a suitcase. "Where do you think you're going?" she asked. "Chicago," he said, defiantly. "I just read in the paper that men have gotten so scarce out there that women are paying them $2.00 to act as gigolos." Mrs. Jaxon nodded her head up and down a few times without saying anything. A few minutes later Mr. Jaxon found that his wife also was throwing her belongings into a valise.

"Where are you bound for?" he asked. "I'm going to Chicago, too," said Mrs. Jaxon, "I just want to see how you are going to manage to live on $4.00 a month."

CUTIE   A certain neighbor of ours has the cutest little baby boy. He is only about three months old, but you ought to see the little chap's muscles. He has the strongest arms, and the hardest little stomach. And bawls . . . why he bawls all day.

PROUD PAPA   A young mother came to the door of the nursery and saw her husband standing over the baby's crib. Silently and motionless she continued to watch him as he stood looking down at the sleeping infant. In his face she read rapture, doubt, admiration, ecstasy, incredulity, wonder. Deeply touched and with her eyes glistening she tip-toed up to her husband and slipped her arm around him.

"A penny for your thoughts," she said tenderly. Startled into consciousness, Harry blurted, "For the life of me I don't see how the furniture store can sell a crib like that for $8.49."

ENOUGH'S ENOUGH A man, suspecting his wife of infidelity, hired a detective to shadow her.

After a few days the detective discovered the wife in her own room with a boy friend in an exceptionally fond embrace on the divan. Quickly locating the husband, he brought him to the home where both peeked in through the door and found the couple still making love.

Visibly shocked, the husband invited the detective into the kitchen, saying: "Let's have some coffee while I think."

The detective replied: "Certainly, thanks, but just make me one cup. That's all I'm allowed."

"Sure," said the husband, "that's enough for me, too."

So they retired to the kitchen where the husband silently brewed two steaming cups of coffee. As they sat down to drink, the detective broke the silence: "Well, what about the fellow in there?"

Replied the husband: "Oh, the hell with him; let him make his own coffee."

SHAME! The farm had been mortgaged to give daughter a college education. Father drove the old model T to the station to pick her up after the graduation exercises. She climbed in beside him, glancing at his worn shirt and clean but patched overalls, sighed and then snuggled close to the good old man.

"Dad, I'm sorry, but I have a confession to make," she whispered, "I ain't a virgin no more."

The old man stopped, wrung his hands, dropped his head in shame and a tear welled up in his eye. "To think that after all our sacrifice you still say 'ain't'!"

POSITION IS EVERYTHING

G. I. Joe married Suzie Cue. Suzie's parents induced them to spend the honeymoon at the parents' home. About midnight, Suzie said quietly to Joe, "I can't sleep. Let's pack and leave."

Joe said, "Okay."

They crammed everything in a suitcase and Suzie said to Joe a little loudly, "Get on top and push." It wouldn't close.

Then Joe said, "Let's both get on top."

All of a sudden, the light was clicked on and Suzie's father, in the doorway, said, "This, I must see."

TOO YOUNG AND TOO OLD

An old man, walking down the street, saw a small boy sitting on the curb crying. He stopped and asked, "Little boy, what are you crying about?" The little boy said, "I'm crying because I can't do what the big boys do." So, the old man sat down alongside and cried too.

OOMPOSSIBLE

One of our friends was describing Lady Luck to his girl.

"You see," he explained, "she has dice for earrings, and eight-balls for a bra—"

The girl's eyes opened wide as she gasped.

"My God—eight?"

3'S A CROWD

Overheard in a Pullman traveling between Chicago and New York:

"I'm deeply sorry, ladies, I'm a married man, a man of respect and standing in my community. I cannot have a breath of scandal touch me. I am sorry, but . . . one of you girls will have to leave."

"Of course they float! What'd you think?"

BED AND BOARD   A retired Minnesota farmer, affectionately known as "Daddy" to most of the residents of the small community in which he lived, had been "batching" it for several years since his wife's death. A trusted attorney took care of most of his affairs and for the most part he had not a care in the world.

One day Daddy went to see his attorney. "I'm going to get married again," he said, "I'm tired of living alone."

"That's probably all right," said the lawyer, "whom do you intend to marry?"

"Leona Mitchell," said Daddy, "I've already asked her."

"Why that won't do," replied the attorney—"That just can't work out. She's much too young for you. Let's see, how old is Leona now?"

"Just turned twenty-two," responded the old man.

"You can't do that, Daddy," explained the attorney, "young gals that age have to have plenty of love and attention and you're just too old for that sort of thing."

But the old man was adamant and would not be swerved from his intention. Come hell or high water he was going to marry Leona and that was that. Realizing that the old man meant exactly what he said the attorney continued with his wise counsel. "All right, Daddy, if that's the way you feel go right ahead. However, if I were you I think I'd take in a good looking roomer. You've got plenty of space in the old house and then maybe your wife would be better satisfied."

"I'll do it!" said Daddy.

Time went by. It was probably six months later when the attorney greeted Daddy on the street and asked how everything was going. "Never happier

(Next Page)

in my life," said Daddy, "and my wife's going to have a baby!"

"Oh," exclaimed the attorney with a knowing sort of look in his eye, "and how about the roomer?"

"Still with us," proudly announced Daddy, "and she's going to have one, too!"

WELL? A girl applied for a job, and was sent to the personnel department, presided over by a large, rather handsome man at a big desk. She was given a form to fill out, and retired to a table in a corner of the room with it.

Most of the blanks she filled out with no great difficulty, but presently he noticed that she seemed to be having trouble in deciding how to answer one question. She looked him over furtively, chewed the pen, then wrote a word or two and brought over the card.

He looked it over casually — name, age, address, telephone number; then came a space which said: "Sex . . ." Here she had written: "Occasionally."

AND HOW Two patients in a hospital were exceedingly bored. They found a stack of diagnosis cards in a corner and began a game of poker. One shuffled the cards and dealt. They picked up their hands and looked at the cards. One bet, the other raised and they raised and reraised until one finally called.

"Looks like I win. I've got three pneumonias and two gallstones."

"Not so fast. Not so fast. I've got four enemas."

"Well, I guess you take the pot."

THE SDIRTY OAK   It seems that a little tree only a few feet high growing at the edge of the forest was the butt of curiosity and discussion of everyone strolling by. "My, what kind of tree is this?" people would say. "I don't know," was the usual reply, "but it sure is a funny little tree." The poor little thing was really developing an inferiority complex and one day after hearing many such remarks, the little tree turned to the big oak standing a few yards away and said, "Mr. Oak, you are a wise old man, can you tell me whether I am a son of a beech or a son of a birch?" The old oak looked down at the little tree and said, "I am sorry that I can't tell you whether you are a son of a beech or a birch, but there is one thing I can tell you — your mother was the finest piece of ash in this neck of the woods."

COMPENSATION   Then there's the stenographer who had to take three pay cuts. On the first she cut out her dollar lunches, on the second she gave up nylon hose and on the third she lost her amateur standing.

EVEN   A stenographer who was struck on the shoulder by a flying paper clip, decided to visit the company doctor. It was her first visit there, and being naturally shy, she hesitated a while before going over to a middle-aged man, explained her trouble and asked him to examine her shoulder. He responded agreeably, and began to examine her thoroughly. It was not long until the blushing young maiden looked down and said, "But Doctor, that isn't my shoulder you're examining."

"That's all right," he said, "I'm not the Doctor."

"Let's slip upstairs and get our
things together."

EXTRA CURRICULAR

One time there was a young man with an apartment, and to this apartment he would bring young ladies (among others). On the particular night in question, he brought a very fair one indeed. He sat down in a chair and turned on soft music. "Have a cigarette," he said politely. "No thanks." Taken somewhat aback, he opened the liquor cabinet. "Have a drink," he said politely. "No thanks." He gave up. Reaching for her coat, he walked toward the door. "Well, may as well be getting you home. Unless," he said politely, "you would care to spend the night right here." "Don't mind if I do," she said. The next morning he looked across the toaster with a puzzled expression. "Last night," he said, "I would have bet a hundred dollars you weren't this sort." "Well," she said with a yawn, "It's just like I've been telling my School class. You don't have to smoke and drink to have a good time."

SH-H

A foreign diplomat was sitting beside a very beautiful blonde who possessed all the social graces. During the course of the dinner, he put his hand under the table and started to feel her ankle.

She gave him a brilliant smile. Encouraged, he went a little further and reached the calf of her leg with the same results. The lady smiled and he, becoming emboldened with this encouragement, went above the knees.

Very soon, giving the diplomat a lovely smile she leaned and whispered in his ear: "When you get far enough to discover that I'm a man, don't change the expression on your face — I'm Secret Agent No. 13."

"Don't sweetheart me, you doublecrosser! You said that we were only going to wrestle!"

TALE OF A TUB A big city steno, vacationing in the country, went swimming in the raw in a secluded mill pond. Along came Ron Denk who tied knots in her clothes. She flopped around, found an old wash tub, held it up in front of her, and marched toward him, saying, "You nasty man, do you know what I'm thinking?" "Sure," said Ron. "You're thinking that that tub has a bottom in it!"

OVER THE WAVES A Wave, very much in love with two sailors, could not decide which one she would marry. Finally, she just put out to sea.

SHADY BUT CLEAN A traveling salesman had spent a few days in Chicago. Shortly after checking out of his hotel he discovered that he had left his umbrella behind and went back to recover the lost article.

Just as he was about to try the door of his room he overheard the conversation of some newlyweds inside.

"Whose little eyebrows are those?"

"Yours."

"Whose little eyes are those?"

"Yours."

"Whose little nose is that?"

"Yours."

"Whose little lips are those?"

"Yours."

"And whose little neck?"

"Yours."

At this point the salesman could stand it no longer. "Hey," he shouted, "when you come to an umbrella, that's mine!"

"I'll tell Miss Tritz you're here, she's taking a bath right now sir."

SLOW DOWN We know a girl who is very slow. So slow in fact, that she went into a grocery store and took twenty minutes to decide between dried prunes and dried apricots. The grocer became impatient and told her to hurry as he had other customers waiting.

"Oh," she said, "if you think I'm slow, you ought to see my sister. She was out with a boy friend last night and while she was trying to explain that she was not that kind of girl; she was."

MEOW The young doctor was taking his wife out one evening, when a pretty girl smiled and spoke to him. The wife scenting an earlier love affair, inquired: "Who is the lady, dear?"

"Oh, just a girl I have met professionally."

"No doubt," meowed the wife, "but whose profession? Yours or hers?"

TEE-HEE One night the farmer's son went to the city, and in search of feminine company he wandered into a bar. At one table sat an attractive, well-dressed blonde. He went over to the table. Her manner was very cool and haughty, but under the spell of his frank, boyish charm, she relented, and permitted him to buy her a drink.

They finished the cocktail, and he ordered another. Cocktail followed cocktail until the farmer's son — whose capacity was quite limited — looked at the blonde and shook his head doubtfully.

"I dunno," he said. "Another one of these and I'm afraid I'm gonna feel it."

"Another one of these," she giggled, "and I'm afraid I'm going to let you."

DROOPY   "Didja hear about the sleepy bride who couldn't stay awake for a second?"

CUSTOMER'S WAYS WRITE   The following is a copy of correspondence between Mr. X and the Philadelphia Transit Company. (We doubt very much if this was actually written to the Philadelphia Company but permit it to stay in because Philadelphia is one of the few cities that has subways.)

The Philadelphia Transit Co.

Gentlemen:

I've been riding your subways for the past two years and I think the service gets worse every day. I think the service you offer is worse than that enjoyed by the people 1,000 years ago.

> Yours truly,
> Mr. X.

Reply—

Dear Mr. X:

We have your letter and are convinced that you are somewhat confused in your history. The only transportation offered 1,000 years ago was afoot.

> Very truly yours,
> Philadelphia Transit Co.

Answer—

Gentlemen:

In receipt of your letter, but believe me you are the ones confused in your history. If you read the Bible you'll find in the book of David, 9th Verse: "Aaron rode into town on his ass." That, gentlemen, is something I have been unable to do for the past eight or ten months.

> Very truly yours,
> Mr. X.

JUST AN OLD COW-POKE   A little country lad accompanied his father on an expedition to buy a new cow. The father gave his prospective purchase a going-over from head to foot, poking, probing, and pinching the animal very thoroughly. "You see, son," he explained, "when you buy a cow you want to be sure it's a sound one." The boy nodded approval. A week later the boy came running breathlessly to his father in a distant corner of the farm. "Come quick, pa," he entreated. "A traveling salesman's pulled up behind the barn, and it looks like he's going to buy Sister."

UNCANNY   Little Audrey nailed the bathroom door shut and then laughed and laughed, because she knew her father was having a beer party at the house that night.

DOUBLE TROUBLE   Two acquaintances were walking down the street when one noticed two women approaching. "My God," said one. "Here comes my wife and mistress, together." The other man looked up and said, "Good heavens, you took the words right out of my mouth."

POLITE   A clergyman and a truck driver found themselves in an automobile smashup. The truck driver told the padre what he thought about him in profane terms. When he paused for breath it was the clergyman's turn. "You know, my good man, that I cannot indulge in your kind of language, but this much I will tell you: I hope when you get home tonight, your mother will run out from under the porch and bite you."

"That babe made quite an impression on me."

VIRGIN HAM A Hollywood director, displeased with a performance, ranted about the cast's lack of acting ability. In his rage he even denounced their moral character. At this, the leading lady stalked haughtily off the set.

She returned the next day and thrust a document under the director's nose.

"What's this?" he cried.

"A medical certificate attesting to my virginity," she sneered.

"But it's no good," said the director, "It's dated yesterday!"

STORMY WEATHER Once during a severe rain storm, three roosters found themselves caught in the deluge. Two of them ran for the barn. The third, and smartest one, made a duck under the porch.

HIGHER LEARNING Dr. Jaxon, a distinguished member of the faculty at a Western University had finished lecturing a class on anatomy and began to ask questions. "I would like to know," he said, looking over the young men and women sitting eagerly before him, "what part of the human body is harder than steel?" Pointing to a pretty Mexican lass, he asked, "Will you answer, Miss LaPido?"

Poor Miss LaPido blushed and stuttered and ended by saying indignantly: "I don't know why I should be selected to answer such a question."

Dr. Jaxon asked a few other pupils, and could get no satisfactory reply. "Since none of you seem to know, I will tell you," he said. "It is the tissue from which the nails of the human body grow. As for you, Miss LaPido, you're an optimist."

COME Y'OUT　　An old maid who possessed several million dollars and a pedigreed female cat, also possessed very Victorian ideas on the subjects of modern living and sex. In fact, her ideas on sex were such that for five years she had never allowed her cat to go out of the house for fear of "contamination."

Deciding to take a vacation, she instructed her housekeeper, while waiting for the train. "You understand everything that must be done while I am gone. Just one more thing. Don't let the cat out. I repeat, under any circumstances, do not let the cat out."

After the old lady had been gone about a week, the housekeeper received a telegram: "Having a wonderful time. Met the nicest young man. LET THE CAT OUT!"

RESTRICTED　　Then there was the boastful Blond who bragged that her husband had never found a stranger in her closet—they were all his friends.

TORPEDOED　　When leaving his house one morning, a certain young man gulped down his breakfast, grabbed his hat, kissed his wife and said "Goodbye, dear!"

His wife said, "Goodbye, Jap!"

When he got to the office and was thumbing through the morning mail, it suddenly dawned on him what his wife had said and he couldn't understand why she called him Jap. He phoned her finally and said, "Dear, didn't you call me Jap when I left this morning and why?"

She said: "Yes, because of that sneak attack before dawn this morning."

MY-AM-I? When a top salesman of a large New York firm went on his honeymoon, he and his bride traveled south on a train that ran through Florida. As the train neared the state, he was in the washroom shaving and at the same time conversing with a fine old southern gentleman with whom he had struck up an acquaintanceship.

"You all just married, ain't you?" queried the southerner with a grin.

"Yes, my dear man," answered the groom nervously cutting his lip with the razor, "my wife and I plan to honeymoon in Florida."

"Are you all going to Tampa with her?" further inquired the gentleman.

The groom bristled, "You're darn tootin' I am, but what the hell is it to you?"

CURIOUS A social worker hearing that a group of refugees would be brought to a nearby church, got into her car and rushed to the spot. Soon a truck appeared laden with people. Clinging together on the edge of the crowd were an old man and old woman.

"You two," she said, "would you like to come home with me?"

After a hasty consultation, they said they would be delighted and she took them to her house, gave them a good meal, and showed them to the guest room. In a few moments the little old lady appeared. Very humble she was, and most grateful for all the attentions she had had, but would the kind lady be good enough to answer one question?

Of course she would.

"Well, then, please tell me who is this old man I'm supposed to sleep with?"

"Who the hell asked for help!"

PLATONIC A young couple got married and directly after the ceremony, left for a honeymoon trip. When they arrived at a resort village in the mountains they decided to stay for a short while at a summer hotel. Upon their arrival they employed a bellhop to look after their baggage, the bridegroom giving him explicit instructions about removing all the rice and labels from their trunks so that no one would know that they were newlyweds. He tipped the 'hop generously to insure against that worthy letting the news leak out that they were just married.

Two or three days later, whenever the bride left her room she noticed that everyone rushed to get a view of her. She informed her husband of the strange actions and he, feeling sure the bellhop had broken his word, called the latter to his room.

"What does this mean? I told you to be particularly careful about not letting people discover that we were just recently married. You were the only one who knew. Now how does it happen that everyone gapes at us, and that all those old girls on the front porch are continually whispering when we appear?"

"Honest to goodness, boss I ain't told nobody at all that you was just married. The fact is, that I told 'em just the opposite. I told 'em you wasn't married a-tall, but just good friends."

BUSY-BUSY A sweet young thing visiting Brooklyn's Zoo in Prospect Park one Sunday asked the keeper where the monkeys were.

Keeper: "They're in the back, making love."

Sweet young thing: "Would they come out for some peanuts?"

Keeper: "Would you?"

"Professor Lampert claims to have invented a mechanical woman!"

IT'S A VIRTUE   A widower and his son ran a dairy farm several miles from a small city. One Saturday night the son finished his chores, changed his clothes, and drove into town. Next morning just before milking time, he drove into the yard, dashed into the house, changed into his work clothes and hurried back to the barn to help his father.

When his father began to protest against his late hours, the boy said—"Don't be hard on me, dad. Last night I was out with a very passionate woman."

The next Saturday night the old man went to town. Milking time had come and gone the next morning before the father finally drove into the farmyard. As the boy started to protest at having to do all the chores by himself, the old man said:

"Don't be too hard on your old dad, boy. Last night I was out with a very PATIENT woman."

NATIONAL PASTIME   "They must have a girl's ball team in the harem."

"What makes you think so?"

"I just heard one of the girls ask the Sultan if she was in tomorrow's line-up."

UNCERTAIN   A local lawyer was sitting in his office the other morning when in walked a beautiful young lady. Without any preliminaries she said she wanted a divorce.

"On what grounds?" asked the lawyer.

"I don't think he is faithful to me," she replied.

"And what makes you think he isn't faithful?" asked the lawyer.

"Well," replied the young lady, "I don't think he is the father of my child."

"Don't you ever get tired of the same two lumps every morning?"

WATCH OUT   A young school teacher had been telling her class about the value of being observant and said, "Now, children, look at the clock; what does the clock have that I have, too?"

One girl stood up and said, "It has a face." Another girl raised her hand and said, "It has hands."

"Splendid," said the teacher, "now what has the clock got that I haven't?"

After a long silence, a boy rose and said, "You ain't got no pendulum."

SMUGGLED   A man with a very small puppy in his arms attempted to board a train in a small Wyoming town. The conductor saw the dog and denied the man entrance to the coach unless he took the pup to the baggage car. The man walked down the train a ways, unbuttoned his coat and shirt and tucked the little dog inside. All this was observed by a lady passenger through the window of the car.

Once again the man attempted to board the train, this time with success, since the pup was not within sight of the conductor. Unfortunately the man with the dog took the seat ahead of the woman who had seen him hide it.

The train pulled out of the station. In a few minutes the man commenced to wiggle around nervously in his seat. As he twisted this way and that the woman could not help but find amusement in his evident discomfiture. Thinking to tease the man about his hidden secret, the woman leaned forward, tapped the man on the shoulder, and inquired: "What's the matter? Isn't he housebroken?"

"Don't know about that," answered the man grimly, "but I don't believe the little cuss has ever been weaned."

YES AND NO   A none too brilliant witness was on the stand testifying to the character of a woman whose reputation was not all that it should have been.

Said the prosecuting attorney: "How about the veracity of this witness?"

The man on the stand scratched his head and answered: "W-a-l-l, some sez she does and some sez she don't."

TOUCHING   Then there was the backward boy who refused to work in a kitchen. He has a good reason, he says, because he heard about a cook who got his hand caught in a dishwasher — and they were both fired.

ALL SIZES   A local dispenser of ladies shoes placed the following sign in his window:

"FRENCH HEELS
GOOD FOR STREET WALKING."

CUT SHORT   Husband: "After I get up in the morning and shave, I feel ten years younger."

Wife: "Why don't you try shaving before you go to bed?"

BELLY LAUGH   The couple were huddled together very closely. The lights were low — very low. He pressed his lips into her shell-like ear and whispered, "What are you thinking about, Darling?"

"The same thing you are, my pet," she shyly answered.

"Then I'll race you to the ice-box!" he shouted.

ROOM AND BROAD A traveling salesman was about to check in at a hotel when he noticed a very charming bit of femininity giving him the so-called "glad-eye."

In a casual manner he walked over and spoke to her as though he had known her all his life. Both walked back to the desk and registered as Mr. and Mrs.

After a three-day stay he walked up to the desk and informed the clerk that he was checking out. The clerk presented him with his bill for $250.

"There's a mistake here," he protested. "I have been here only three days."

"Yes," replied the clerk, "but your wife has been here a month."

NOSEY A midget was kicked out of the nudist colony because he had his nose in everybody's business.

WHAT'S UP DOC? They'd only been married the night before and now it was Sunday morning. He woke up, stretched and said, "Gosh, I can lie in bed now. I don't have to go to work today. I'd love to have my breakfast in bed — would you mind too much, Dear?"

The wife hopped out of bed with alacrity and soon returned carrying a tray upon which there was a large bowl of raw carrots, garnished with a head of lettuce.

He protested. "I thought I was going to get a real breakfast — coffee, rolls, bacon and eggs. What's the meaning of this?"

"Oh, nothing," she replied, "but seeing the way you make love I thought perhaps you ate like a rabbit, too."

PROGRESS   The difference between the old saloon and a modern night club is that in the old time saloon a wistful little girl would pull on your sleeve and whisper, "Daddy, dear Daddy, come home with me now," and you wouldn't pay any attention to her.

In a night club now a wistful little girl pulls at your sleeve and whispers, "Daddy, dear Daddy, come home with me now," and you do.

APPRECIATIVE   One morning a young fellow boarded a commuter train up in Connecticut for New York. He stopped beside a gentleman reading a newspaper in the seat next to the window. "Pardon me," he said to the reader, "do you mind if I lean across you and open the window? I want to speak to a man on the platform."

"Go ahead." And he pulled his paper close to his face to make room.

The young man shoved the window up and shouted, "Hey, Charlie!" Charlie came over to the window, and the fellow said, "Thanks a lot for inviting me up to your country place for the week-end. You certainly have a beautiful place up here. I don't know when I've had a better time. Your wife is really a good cook, and, incidentally, she's the best bed partner I ever had." With this he slammed the window and sat down.

The old gent with the paper blinked his eyes, and wondered if he could possibly have heard the conversation correctly. Finally he could stand it no longer, so he put his paper down, and turned to the young man beside him. "Your pardon, but did I understand you to say you spent the week-end up here with Charlie?"

(Next Page)

"That's right," his seat-mate replied.

"And that Charlie's place is very beautiful, and that you had a good time?"

"A lovely place, and I don't think I ever had a better time."

"You think Charlie's wife is a good cook?"

"I've never known a better one."

"And did I really hear you say she's the best bed-partner you ever had?"

"Well, confidentially, she isn't. But Charlie's such a good friend of mine I didn't want to hurt his feelings."

HIRSUTE A maiden lady engaged a local carpenter to erect a small outhouse on her premises. After a few days, she called the carpenter and asked him to come over for the purpose of remedying a defect in its construction. "What's the trouble?" he asked upon arriving. "The half moon over the door seems all right." "T'aint that," she simpered. "The roof is sound," he continued and enumerated, item by item, the outer structural elements. In each case her laconic answer was, "T'aint that." Entering, he made a thorough inspection of the interior. "The hinges are all right and the door stays shut." "T'aint that," was again the rejoinder. The inspection of the interior completed, he stuck his head down one of the openings in the seat in order to make a complete survey. As he withdrew his head, he caught a wisp of his whiskers in a minute crack in the seat. "Ouch!" he said.

"Good," she cried, "That happened to me twice this week!"

WATTAMAN   An 80-year-old man went to his doctor for a blood test and medical examination before getting married.

The doctor checked him over, then asked, "You mean at your age you really want to get married?"

The old man replied, "Well, I don't exactly want to. I've got to."

NEW FEELING   An old maid after years and years was invited out to have a date with a man. The next day a friend asked how she enjoyed the evening.

"Fine," she replied smilingly, "it was the first time I ever knew you could have fun without laughing."

REAL LIVE   A certain Big Time Operator came home one evening and raved about his new secretary. She was so efficient and good looking besides.

"Really a doll," he said.

His little daughter spoke up, "Does she close her eyes when you lay her down, daddy?"

P'TUI   It was during prohibition. The railroad station was packed with a gay throng. Over at one side of the waiting room stood a quiet little man fidgeting about, and attempting to hide himself from the crowd. A federal agent noticed that the man had something in his pocket from which drops were falling in slow trickles. The fed, with a gleam in his eye, put a finger out under one of the drops, caught one and tasted it.

"Scotch?" he asked.

"Nope," replied the stranger, "Airdale pup."

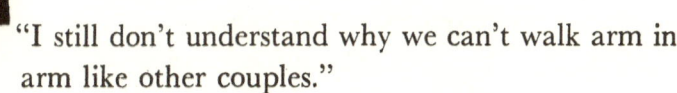

"I still don't understand why we can't walk arm in arm like other couples."

TALL TALE Mac and Paddy were swimming down the East River in a race from Forty-second Street to South Ferry. They swam steadily along until Paddy started thinking about his date that night with his beautiful Bridget. Turning about Mac saw his friend floundering about on one spot. "What's the trouble?" he asked. "I'm stuck in the mud," shouted Paddy. "Why don't you turn over and float awhile," suggested Mac. "Yea," bellowed Paddy, "but what'll I do when I get to the Brooklyn Bridge?"

SMOOTH A certain character was having his ears lowered in his neighborhood shop, when the barber said loudly, "Do you know, your head feels just like my wife's cheek."

"By George, it does, doesn't it?" came the reply.

SAVE A PENNY, BENNY Joe had a very homely wife. One day he came home earlier than usual and found her in the arms of his friend Benny. He watched them hugging and kissing for a few minutes, then cried, "Listen, Benny, I MUST—but YOU?"

YIPEE Red Diamond, recently in Oklahoma, had difficulty getting a hotel room and shared one with a cowboy from Texas. One morning, about a week later, the cowboy was in the bathroom shaving when Red entered. Red then placed the toilet seat in position and the Texan turned and said:

"Huh, I didn't know they had a saddle for that thing! I've been riding it bare-back ever since we've been here."

144

"Guess what — Junior learned how to multiply today!"

OOPS

"Doctor," said the young lady, "there's something wrong with our baby's diet. He doesn't gain as he should, what would you suggest?"

"Is he a bottle fed baby?" asked the doctor.

"Nn-n-n-n-n-o."

"Well, we'd better make an examination," said the doctor, cheerfully — (pause) — "There, does that hurt?"

"N-n-n-n-n-o, I guess it feels all right," said the girl uncertainly — "but doctor — I'm the baby's aunt!"

WHAT A KISSER

A sweet young thing was entertaining a hot date in the parlor of her home and the guy started to close in on her.

"If you kiss me," she warned, "I'll call a member of my family."

So he kissed her.

"Bro-ther!" she whispered.

SQUEEZA DA ORANGE

Doctor: "Young lady, I can not ethically or legally give you the information for which you ask. However, I suggest the use of orange juice —"

Bride (interrupting): "Before or after?"

Doctor: "Neither, my dear girl — instead of!"

BLOW YE WINDS

A woman in the windy city was seen holding her hat with both hands while her skirt blew higher and higher. In response to the quizzical glances of male passersby she sagaciously commented . . . "Gentlemen, what you are looking at is 40 years old. What I'm hanging onto is brand new!"

"You wouldn't buy a car without driving it first, would you?"

EXPLORED Once upon a time there was a boy penguin and a girl penguin who met at the equator. After a brief but charming interlude, the boy penguin went north to the north pole and the girl penguin went south to the south pole. Later a telegram arrived at the North Pole, stating simply: COME QUICK I AM WITH BYRD.

LABELED "Do you know how to tell a little girl sardine from a little boy sardine?"
"No."
"Look and see which can they come out of."

FRIEND IN-DEED Ivan Petroffsky, a soldier in Stalin's army, returned home to Moscow after spending four years in the army and during all that time, not having seen his wife once. Upon returning home, Sonia, his wife, proudly informed him that he was father of a two year old boy. For a moment Ivan was deliriously happy until he stopped to think.
"For four year I'm being away and I' de Pappa of a two year old boy?" He mused, "Somet'ink is wrong! Aha!"
He advanced on his wife. "So," he sneered, "making de monkey business behind mine back, who was it?" His wife shrank up against the wall and made no answer. Ivan sneered again. "I know! It must have been one of my friends. But who? Could be Alex? Could be Vasiloffsky? It must be one of my friends."
His wife stood in the corner. "Your friends, your friends," she snorted. "Don't you t'ink I got any friends?"

AT THE DEUCE   A newly-wed soldier wrote the following letter to his young bride: "Come down next Sunday if you possibly can. I'm short of cash, so please bring me $10.00. (P.S.—If you can't come send me $12.00)."

ENGROSSED   Gaston had left his lifelong friend, to keep his wife out of other men's arms while he went on a business tour. He trusted him implicitly, but as so often happens in such cases he arrived home unexpectedly and found his friend and wife in the very act that he had asked Alphonse to keep his wife from doing. He upbraided his wife, calling her this and that and the other. Then he gazed with sorrowful eyes at Alphonse: "And you, my friend," he said, "might at least have the courtesy to stop while I'm talking to you."

RY CONTRARY   Two men and a young lady were on the Pullman going to California and decided they had better get acquainted.

One man said: "My name is Paul, but I'm not an Apostle."

The other said: "My name is Peter, but I'm not a saint."

The girl muttered: "My name is Mary, and I don't know what the hell to say."

BOINNNGGG   Lotty: "My husband gave me one of those new electric blankets. It's wonderful. You ought to get one."

Dotty: (who believes the honeymoon is over when a quickie before dinner is a dry martini) "Humph, I'd rather have my husband recharged."

**TOO MUCH-
TOO LATE**   Two men were discussing the use of the English language and the one felt very strongly that it might be embarrassing or even dangerous to use a high sounding word unless you were darn sure of its meaning. To illustrate his argument he cited the case of a backwoodsman who excitedly entered a surgeon's office and panted, "Doctor, I want you to castrate me."

"What?" questioned the doctor, "a husky fellow like you?"

"Don't ask any questions, Doc," the other answered, "just castrate me. Here's your money."

Shrugging his shoulders, the doctor called his assistant who administered the ether, and the patient lost the power of his sex. As he came out of the ether, the doctor leaned over and said, "While you're on the table, why not be circumsized?"

"Dawgone it, Doc," said the patient in a squeaky voice, "that's the word I wanted. That's what I wanted done!"

PIZEN   Before John Doe had become a Big Time Operator in the Army Air Force in the last war, he had taken his basic training in Florida where things were pretty rough. He still tells about the time the Colonel ordered him to go down to the river for some drinking water.

John went off, but came back, post haste.

"Colonel " he exclaimed, "there's a big alligator in the river, and I'm afraid to get the water."

The Colonel turned patronizingly to John and said, "Don't worry son, that alligator is probably four times as afraid of you as you are of him."

"Well, sir," John replied, "if that alligator is only half as scared as I am, that water ain't fit to drink."

Martini: "Is that Hortense?"
Pink Lady: "She looks relaxed to me."

A nudist who has just spilled steaming coffee in his lap is next to the fastest thing in the world!

Some fellows like tall girls, others go for those little lasses.

"Mommy, I just came in to kiss you goodni . . ." "MOMMY!"

He: "How many beers does it take to make you dizzy?"
She: "About four or five, and don't call me dizzy."

Remember the good old days when silk stockings were within the reach of all.

It was said of a certain erotomaniac that he had love on his mind so much that regularly every month he had a nosebleed!

She: "It's shameful the way you start making passes at me after a half-dozen drinks."
He: "What's shameful about that?"
She: "Wasting five drinks."

"He made a perfect thirty-six on the golf course today."
"Nine holes?"
"No, Fifth Avenue model."

Mistress: Something between a mister and a mattress.

The buxom soprano in the opera fainted and it required four men to carry her off the stage . . . Two abreast.

There was a little country girl who came to college and always went out with city fellers because farm hands were too rough.

Have you heard about the absent-minded nurse who made the patient without disturbing the bed?

Definition of a jitterbug: A man with a wife, a girl friend, and a note at the bank, all a month past due.

. . . And then there is the widow who wears black garters in remembrance of those who have passed beyond.

"What was the most exciting event in your family, Johnny?"
Johnny—"When Sister Mister • "

If you love me,
Like I love you,
Then shame on us!

As the little dog said, while walking through the tobacco patch, "Does your cigarette taste different lately?"

"Okay, Baby, are you going to give me a kiss?"
"Make me!"
"All I want is a kiss."

She was the kind of a girl you'd like to bring home to mother, if you could trust father.

"Huh?"
"Uh-huh!"

Simpson (on phone)—Say, I got a leak in my basement!
Plumber—Well, go ahead; it's your basement!

Said the beautiful girl to her beau: "So far and no father."

Confucius say—Man who lose key to girl's apartment get no new key.

She: "Oh look—the bridesmaid!"
He: "My gosh, so soon?"

Women are like potatoes; when they're big enough, they're old enough.

She was so innocent she wouldn't molest a fly unless it was open.

When it got dark he turned to Kitty and said: "You know, darling, I can't see my hand in front of me."
"Don't worry," she said, "I know where it is."

BUSHED   It was the morning after their wedding the night before. The groom arose, walked over to the window and raised the shade. The day was dark and gloomy and the rain was falling in torrents. Disgusted, he lowered the shade and climbed back into bed.

The next morning the young groom rose again and lifted the shade. It was still raining. He once more lowered the shade and crawled back in bed.

The third morning he got out of bed, went over to raise the shade — and went up with it.

SAME DIFFERENCE   A professor in English was asked by some students to define the difference between fornication and adultery.

"The difference?" said the professor with an absent-minded expression, "I've tried them both and they seem the same to me."

FIELD DAY   The subject of discussion among the girls was the effect of alcohol upon them. One remarked, "If I take one drink, I can feel it. If I take two drinks, I can feel it a little—but if I take three drinks—anybody can feel it."

WHY I HATE MEN   I hate men because they take me into alleys, dance halls, taverns, and bedrooms—They press me and feel me all over with their fingers. After they get me hot, they hold me to their lips and drag the life out of me. When they get what they want they throw me aside and I'm only good for tramps.

Why should they take advantage of my white body? After all, I'm only a cigarette!

"I thought you said this drink would knock my hat off!"

STAND IN   Drunk staggers into bar, struggles up onto bar stool and asks for comfort station. Bartender tells him, and he struggles off stool and starts toward door.
"Go for me while you're there," yells bartender.
Drunk agrees.
After a while he returns to bar; struggles back onto stool.
"XZ&œM!" says drunk, "I forgot." He struggles back off stool and starts for door again.
After a long time he returns to struggle onto stool once more. Glowers at bartender.
"What's the matter," asks B.T.
"You ZœlbœD!" says drunk, "you didn't have to go at all."

WORSER   "What's worse than being a bachelor?"
"Being a bachelor's son."

HEAD OR TAIL?   A gay and unmarried (naturally) fellow became interested in phrenology, the science of telling all about a person by examining the bumps on his head. After trying for a long time, he finally succeeded in making an appointment with a famous phrenologist. The day before his appointment, he was phoned by his sweetie who wanted him to come up and see her the next night.
"I'd love to see you, Honey," he said, "but I've got a date to have my head read."
"Break it," she insisted, "I'll be alone in the apartment tomorrow, and you don't need any fortuneteller to tell you what will be in store for you."
"Gee," he answered, "I don't know what to do."
"Well, Casanova," she replied before hanging up, "I'll tell you how to decide. Toss a coin."

"I still fail to see the advantage Mr. Hechter."

WORRIED "Am I scared! Got a letter from a man saying he'd shoot me if I didn't stay away from his wife."

"Well, all you gotta do is stay away from her."

"Yes, but he didn't sign his name."

CLOSE The good doctor carefully diagnosed the case, then took down from the shelf a large bottle of castor oil, a glass, and a spoon. Setting the glass upon the table and opening the bottle, he asked his patient, "Did you walk here from your home this morning?" When the man nodded, the doctor asked how far his home was from the office.

"Oh, about a mile, I'd say." Into the glass slipped two spoonfuls of the thickish liquid.

"Now," continued the doctor, "About how far is it from your front door to the bathroom?"

"Oh, I'd say about twenty feet," the man answered. The doctor added more to the glass.

"And about how many feet is it to the toilet seat?"

"Oh, about eight, I'd say."

Another tiny portion of castor oil was added to the glass. Then the good doctor instructed the man very carefully.

"Now you drink this down, and walk straight home! Remember, straight home!" The man drank the horrible stuff, paid the doctor and left. An hour later the man called the doctor.

"Doc," came a weak voice, "You sure are a good doctor but a darn poor engineer! You missed it by eleven feet!"

OOH-LA-LA The latest styles in bathing suits at the French Riviera resort consist of two Band-aids and a cork.

FRAME UP The crowd had gathered that evening for no particular reason and were down in Joe's basement recreation room when the subject of conversation got around to most embarrassing moments.

"One time I went to visit friends," said one of the wives, "and during the course of the evening found it necessary to go powder my nose. Now my friend had just redecorated her bathroom with a delightful new color scheme in that new, supposed to be fast drying, glossy plastic enamel. Only this batch didn't seem to have dried fast enough and I found myself stuck. I screamed and in came my friend. She could do nothing and much to my embarrassment, she called to her husband, who at least was able to remove the screws and detach the thing so I could stand up. But we couldn't get it off, so they called the doctor.

'Did you ever see anything like this before?' the doctor was asked when he arrived.

'Yes,' the doc replied, 'but this is the first time I ever saw one framed.' "

STALE-MATE There's the one about the husband who received a card from his wife in the country which read: "Having a wonderful time, dear, wish you were him!"

THE BOTTOM A pregnant woman was told by her doctor that until her child was born she must stop chain-smoking, or suffer what might be serious consequences. The young lady made a valiant effort for a time, but was unable to quit smoking. The months passed, and at last her child was born, and sure enough, there, at the end of the baby's spine, was a little butt.

WALKIE TALKIE Traveling across country, a gentleman stopped at a filling station of a small Missouri town to have a tire changed. As the attendant labored, a lady drove into the station and inquired as to the rest room. "Right out back there at the end of the path," replied the attendant, pointing.

The woman disappeared in the little building at the end of the path and as she closed the door behind her the attendant dropped his tools and headed for the inside of the filling station on a run. In only a moment the door of the little building out back opened violently and here came the lady back to her car as fast as she could go, and arranging her clothing enroute. Her face was crimson red as she slammed the car door and took out of the station in high. The attendant returned to the job on the tire. Soon another woman approached and the performance was repeated. "What's the matter with those women?" asked the gentleman. "They go in and then come back thirty seconds later looking like they're scared to death. What's wrong?"

"Well," explained the Missourian with his southern drawl, "It's like this, Mister. You folks in the city have lots of places to go to have fun and we folks down here have to make our own. Now take that privy down there. I got it wired for sound, Mister, and I have more fun. Every time a lady goes into the place I sneak into the station and pick up the microphone. And I speak into it and say, 'Please move over to the other side, Lady, we're working down here'."

CARELESS Headline in recent N. Y. paper: "Father of Ten Shot; Mistaken for Rabbit."

"See what I mean? Turn 'em upside down and they all look alike."

OVER TRAINED There once was a young, sprightly lad who could make love to two dozen ladies in an hour. A booking agent heard of this feat and offered to put him on the stage to perform to a full house.

The day arrived and the house was jammed. The twenty-four women were all lined up on the stage and out comes this greatest lover of all times. The audience was quiet, not a sound throughout the house. The casanova went to work. He made love to the first ten ladies and then fell to the floor in exhaustion. The manager of the theatre ran out and tried to arouse him. The lover opened his eyes and looked out at the audience and said, "Funny, I can't understand this, I did OK at rehearsal!"

BUM STEER Driver of car asking directions, "I take the next turn don't I?"

Voice from back seat: "Like hell you do, just keep driving."

CLEAN UP A nine year old girl became so enamored of adventure tales and tabloids that she neglected everything to concentrate on reading. Her room became an unholy mess, and all of her mother's exhortations fell on deaf ears.

One afternoon, however, her mother returned home to find her daughter's room as spic-and-span as the operating room of a big hospital. "How wonderful!" she exclaimed. "What got into you?"

"I've realized how important housework is," the daughter informed her. "I read in the paper where two ladies got a year apiece in jail—just for keeping a disorderly house."

NATCH   Question: If the seven dwarfs had a cake cut into seven pieces, but with a single cherry in the center, which one would get the cherry?
Answer: The one who got the first piece.

LUCKY STRIKE   Student: "I want a nice room for me and my wife."
Clerk: "Yes, sir, just sign the register. Anything else?"
Student: "Yeah, gimme a pack of cigarettes."
Clerk: "What brand sir?"
Student: (turning to wife): "What kind of cigarettes do you smoke, babe?"

BUSY BODY   Overheard in the powder-room.
Mae: "Have you heard about Marie having twins?"
Gae: "No, I didn't."
Mae: "Yes, it was quite a surprise. The doctor told her that only happened once in every 15,781 times."
Gae: "My goodness! How do you suppose she ever finds time to do her housework?"

SURE FIRE   A lad from Mahtomedi whose intentions were strictly honorable, was contemplating matrimony. He wanted to propose but didn't know how, so he went to his dad for advice.

"Well, son," said the old man, "I don't know that I can help you much. With me and yer Ma it happened one Sunday evening when yer Ma and me was a-sittin' there on the sofa. We was just a-talkin' and purty soon yer Ma leaned over and whispered something in my ear and I just said, 'The hell you say,' and the next day we was married."

GOOD TIME AND A HALF

The painter at Mrs. D. F.'s house was a magnificent specimen of man. He started to work on the parlor at 9 a.m., his strong arm gliding the brush along the woodwork, effortless.

At 9:15 Mrs. D. F.'s roving eye spotted this Samson. She suggested he drop his work and romance with her. The painter complied, then wiped the lipstick on his sleeve and went back to work.

At 10:30, another suggestion, and more lipstick.

Came noon, and with the whistle the painter took up his lunch pail and sat back to enjoy the meal. At 12:15 Mrs. D. F. beckoned to him again.

Shaking his head sternly, the painter said, "Nope, not this time — lady, I'm on my own time!"

ACCENTUATE THE NEGATIVE

"No," said the centipede, crossing her legs, " a hundred times no!"

OMIT THE FLOWERS

A couple got married and the first night the man came into the bedroom his wife had on a beautiful white satin gown, "Oh, you look too good to touch," he said.

The next night he came home she had on a beautiful blue satin gown, "Oh, you look just marvelous. I just can't touch you."

The next night he came in, she had on a pink satin gown. "O-oh, you look just wonderful, I just can't even think of touching you." The fourth night she had on an old black drabby affair. When he entered he hastily asked, "Why do you have on such a thing as that?"

"Well," she said, "I'm in mourning. Something's dead around here."

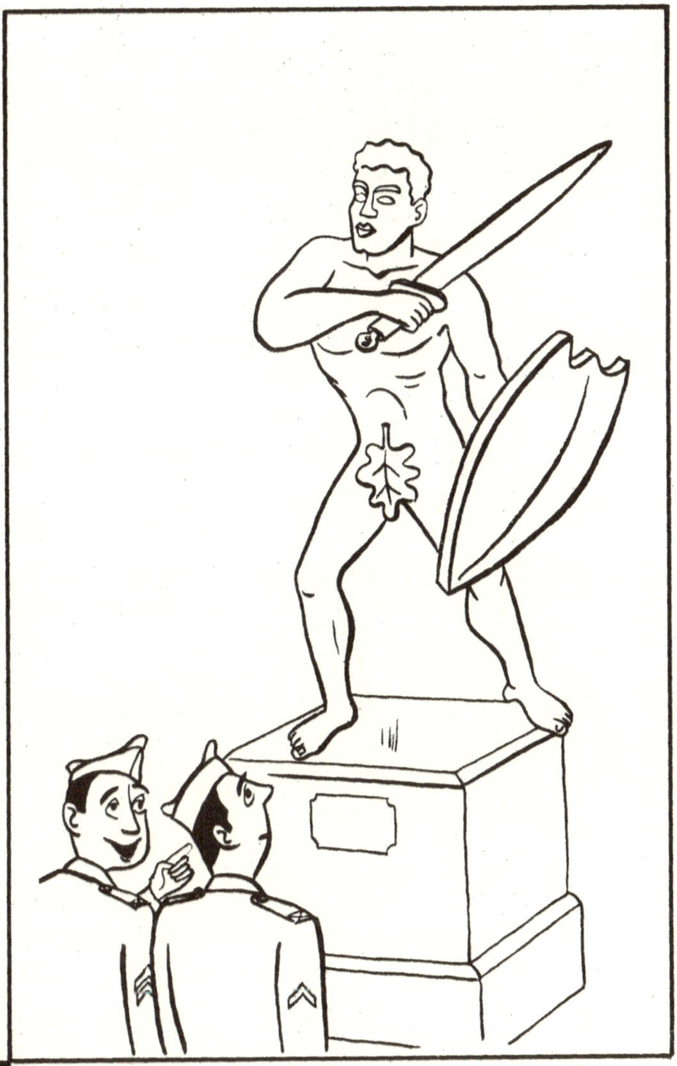

"He must've been a major."

THE CANINE STORY There probably isn't a word of truth in it, but we were told that K. A. Canine was in England some time ago and while there, he taught an English friend to play poker. At one point the Englishman won a big pot. Canine congratulated him by saying, "Lucky Dog."

"My word!" said the limey. "Are you insulting me?"

"Why no," exclaimed his friend. "That's a term of admiration with us, and quite the proper thing to say on an occasion like this."

Some days later, Canine was invited by his English friend to a house party, at which these two joined the host and hostess in a game of bridge. The hostess made a grand slam and raked in the stakes. Admiringly, the Englishman leaned toward her and said, "Lucky Bitch."

HARE-RAISING As one rabbit said to another,
"You've had it."

ABSENT MINDED It seems a certain Professor Tupper was a great hand at exploring and digging in ancient ruins; but when it came to making love, he was a pretty awkward fellow. One night, however, as he rested his head on his beloved's bosom, he felt impelled to express himself.

"You know, dear," he mused happily, "resting here like this gives me great happiness. Only once before in all my life have I felt so relaxed."

"When was that?" asked his girl friend suspiciously.

"One night in Egypt," explained the professor innocently, "when I camped between two of the Pyramids."

Over Sexteen

"If I didn't love you, would I be doing *this*?"

FISHERMAN'S DWARF

It was a foggy morning, and the fishing smacks off Gloucester nosed their way out of the harbor. Suddenly a sailor in one hailed another: "Hello, John, I have news for ye."

"What is it?"

"Wife had a baby, a boy."

"What'd he weigh?" the other voice called.

"Four pounds," came the reply, through the fog.

"Hell, you hardly got your bait back!"

SERVICE

The Blood Collection Center was very busy, and as a nurse rushed out of the room with a container of freshly drawn blood, she met a contractor who was a regular donor. They recognized each other and the nurse greeted the man brightly: "Just jump into bed, sir, I'll be with you in a minute."

CHEERIO

This English sportsman had been abroad and returned to his home without notice. While walking through the corridor with his butler, he looked into his bedroom and discovered his wife making love to a strange man. "Fetch my rifle at once," he instructed his butler. In a matter of minutes his rifle was brought to him and he raised it to his shoulder taking aim, when he was tapped by the butler who whispered, "If I may say so, sir, remember you are a true sportsman. Get him on the rise."

MISTAKES WILL HAPPEN

He: You see, if we enter a companionate marriage we can live together a while and then if we find we've made a mistake we can separate.

She: Yes, but what'll we do with the mistake?

ETIQUETTE An American soldier who was attending a banquet in a London house, given by Lady Brighton, felt quite embarrassed when the lady broke wind. One of the Englishmen rose immediately, said, "I beg your pardon," and sat down. Once more the lady did it and another English guest rose and apologized. "What's the idea?" asked the American of his neighbor.

"Why don't you know? That's the gentlemanly thing to do," said the other.

Again her ladyship let go, but this time the American rose, restraining another Englishman who was about to get up. "I beg your pardon, sir," he said "but this one is on me."

STRAIGHT-FORWARD And then there's the one about the bashful girl who worked all her cross word puzzles vertically so she wouldn't have to come across.

HOARY STORY Mrs. Abigail Sludge, secretary-treasurer of the ladies' bridge and Frank Sinatra club, has a passion for telling "off-color" stories, which were resented by fellow members. One day just before the meeting convened the girls made a pact in which they agreed to leave the room when, and if Mrs. Sludge began her stories. Shortly after the meeting convened Mrs. Sludge settled herself at the bridge table and began, "Girls, did you know that there's a boatload of a thousand prostitutes leaving for Alaska in the morning?" Then, as one, the members of the club rose and headed for the door. "What's the rush, girls? The boat doesn't leave 'til 10 A.M.," retorted Mrs. S.

NEEDS A PUSH It's not because she WOULDN'T
It's not because she SHOULDN'T
It's not because she COULDN'T
She's just the LAZIEST girl in town!

EYE-PATCH The stranger was downing his first drink at the bar
when the voluptuous blonde flung herself upon him.
"Joe! Joey-boy! How are you?"
"I beg your pardon," he answered, "but I'm afraid
I don't know you, lady."
She frowned incredulously. "You don't know me?
Why, Joe! How could you forget me? Joe, you must
remember me! I'm Marge!"
"Gee, lady, you must be taking me for someone else."
"Look," she replied, "Come with me to my place.
You'll be reminded then."
Ready to be convinced, the stranger went up to the
girl's apartment. She shut the door behind them.
"Joe! Doesn't this bring back anything to you?"
"No," he meditated, "I've never been here before."
"Oh, Joe!" the blonde circled her arms around the
man's neck and gave him a long and passionate kiss.
"How about that?" she cooed. "Remember now?"
"I-I'm afraid I don't—" he stammered.
"Wait a second." She slipped out of her dress and
stood in her black bra and panties. "Isn't this even
vaguely familiar to you?"
He shook his head.
The blonde then pulled down one side of her black
brassiere.
"Doesn't this remind you of anything, Joe?"
The man brightened. "Yes, it certainly does!"
"Really, Joe! What?"
"Floyd Gibbons!"

"Quick, ain't he?"

HIDE AND SEEK A farmer was once phoning a veterinarian:
"Say, Doc," he said, "I've got a sick cat. He just lays around licking his paws and doesn't have any appetite; what shall I do for him?"
"Give him a pint of castor oil," instructed the vet. Somewhat dubious, the farmer forced the cat to take a pint of castor oil.
A couple of days later the vet met the farmer on the street.
"How's your sick calf?" inquired the vet.
"Sick calf! That was a sick cat I had."
"My God, did you give him a pint of castor oil?"
"Sure did."
"Well, what did he do?" asked the vet.
"Last I seen him," said the farmer, "he was going over the hill with five other cats. Two were digging; two were covering up; and one was scouting for new territory."

PSYCHIC Chap who joined a nudist club was telling about his first meeting. "They were all quite naked," he said, "even the butler who took my hat and stick." Asked how he knew it was the butler, he snapped . . . "Dammit, I knew it wasn't the maid."

DROP ANCHOR A Sailor who had dropped into one of those Broadway dance palaces was quite struck by one of the pretty hostesses, and gave her a great deal of attention. As they were dancing their last dance, she snuggled up to him and asked, "Aren't you going to take me home, big boy?"
"Is there anything in it," inquired the tar, brusquely.
"Just a little dust from dancing," she answered, coyly.

THE END